Four Guys in a Boat

for Doug
from his mother-in-
law, one of the
4 girls left on the
shore, by "way" :) Dad lived
the "way" — Canada — it is a
it's just Canada — jumping off point.
great jumping off point.
Bon Voyage! Mom
6/30/06

Four Guys in a Boat

A Decade of Rum, Cigars, Poker and Lies

Tom Watkins

Illustrations by Bettyjo Knapp

SHERIDAN HOUSE

Published 2004 by
Sheridan House Inc.
145 Palisade Street
Dobbs Ferry, NY 10522
www.sheridanhouse.com

Library of Congress Cataloging-in-Publication Data
Watkins, Tom
    Four guys in a boat / by Tom Watkins ; illustrations by Bettyjo
  Knapp.
      p. cm.
    Includes bibliographical references.
    ISBN 1-57409-193-X (alk. paper)
      1. Sailing—Caribbean Sea—Anecdotes. 2. Watkins, Tom—
  Travel—Caribbean Sea. I. Title.

GV817.C37W38 2004
797.124'6'09729—dc22   2004017074

ISBN 1-57409-193-X

Printed in the United States of America

To the memory of my wonderful parents,
Bob and Charlotte,
who made everything possible,
and to my incredible wife Linda
who insists I follow my dreams,
and whose love makes them all come true.

Twenty years from now, you will be more disappointed by the things you didn't do than by the ones you did do. So throw off the bowlines. Sail away from the safe harbor. Catch the trade winds in your sails. Explore. Dream. Discover.

—Mark Twain

Contents

Acknowledgments

Clearly the most important people to thank are the other guys who took these trips with me. They contributed not only to my enjoyment and my growth, their recollections were particularly helpful in supplementing my notes of our adventures. I didn't really want to change their names in this book since in the end I think they might actually be proud to be in it, but it's probably useful to protect whatever innocence they may have left.

Bettyjo Knapp was much more than just my illustrator. She provided encouragement and counsel throughout this effort. BJ is not only a fantastic artist and friend, she and her husband Bob are two of our very favorite sailing companions, past and future. Thanks for always being there.

Another person deserving special mention is Lennie Singer—actor, playwright, poet, and former English teacher. She carefully read every draft of the manuscript, offering me the kind of supportive criticism that is simply invaluable. The project would never have been brought to life without her mentoring. Now if we can just find a way to bring this thing to the stage . . .

Harry and Jody Love, partners in our great little MacGregor 26 sailboat, METAFOUR, helped in so many remarkable ways. Harry is the best-read sailor I've ever known; and Jody has been a cheerleader of my stuff for 30 years. They both know sailing inside and out; more importantly, they understand my voice. I deeply appreciate all the evenings they gave up to discuss this manuscript and encourage the pursuit. I treasure their love and support.

Friends Margaret and Bruce Colley, who adore humor, and Rick Hilsabeck, who adores dialogue, and Kirsten Trainor-Smith, who seems to adore manuscripts, also read various incarnations of this effort, and contributed notably to its development.

My wife Linda also read it time after time, telling me candidly what wasn't funny, or what didn't work, or lacked reason. The truth is, she'd rather read than sail. Marriage is, after all, a compromise.

Over the years, I've sailed with dozens of wonderful people each of whom, in one way or another, contributed to my love for the sport. You know who you are. Thanks. You helped make my life richer.

I owe another large debt to the unnamed people all of us met in marinas, restaurants, bars, groceries, and on other boats along the way. Whoever they are and wherever they are, the experiences pale without them.

Finally and critically is the enormous dose of appreciation due the team at Sheridan House for their encouragement—and especially for their willingness to roll the dice with a neophyte.

Without all of these people this collection of wonderful memories would still be in my head rather than on paper. Not a tragedy, certainly; but it gave me a reason to listen rather than teach. That alone is reason for gratitude to all of those who know me.

Introduction

Until a dozen years ago, all my sailing dreams were fairly personal. They didn't involve anyone but me, or maybe my wife Linda and me, possibly another couple or two. I had a few places I wanted to sail, challenges I wanted to address. Emphasis on the word "I."

That all changed when a colleague came into my office and suggested a "guys' trip." Initially I had a lot of ambivalence about that. It didn't square with my sailing fantasies. Sure, I did a lot of guy things: went to football and baseball games, played softball, skied, golfed, sailed locally with guys on my boat. But being cramped together in a small space 24-7? That idea would take some getting used to.

But we *did* go. Over the next decade a bunch of us not only took ten trips together, we lived dreams together.

I made notes on our trips, not for any noble purpose—certainly not because I ever intended to use them as the basis for a book. Nor did I do it out of some lifelong habit. Indeed, I have no such habit even though I routinely tell my MBA students they must keep a journal if they want to learn about themselves, if they seek personal growth. But then part of the satisfaction of teaching comes from telling others to do that which we have no intention of doing ourselves.

No, my reason was far more basic: to be able to create clever captions for the snapshots that Linda selected to put in our photo albums. Two of the other guys jotted some notes too.

Only after the trips ended did I feel compelled to write about them, our adventures and misadventures. We had a blast every time out. Talking about these experiences still brings laughter.

Yet the writing revealed significance we may have missed during the trips themselves: how we felt about each other, about life's challenges, about our dreams.

Everyone dreams. Everyone acts. Sometimes the two aren't connected. What the guys' trips taught us was that dreams matter, whether big or small. But what matters more is *doing* something. Becoming engaged is everything, even if we don't have clarity about what the dream is, or why it is, or how it will change us if we just try to live it.

Sailor Pete Goss once said, "Life hangs on a very thin thread and the cancer of time is complacency. If you are going to do something, do it now. Tomorrow will be too late." We heeded that advice.

Memories followed. And from the memories, often as not, new dreams emerged. Sometimes bigger, always different. Dreams may not change us by themselves but acting on them always does.

As I'm fond of telling my students, "We are far more likely to act our way into new ways of thinking, than to think our way into new behaviors."

For whatever reasons, and they were different, the guys just went. And we had one helluva lot of fun.

Four Guys in a Boat

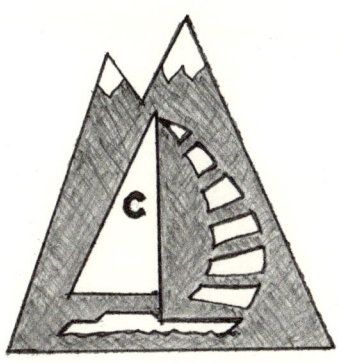

Prologue

There must be more to sailing than the mere setting out to sail from A to B via C. There must be exploration, not only of new areas of the ocean, but also of new parts of yourself.

—Tristan Jones

t was all Tania's fault. My colleague and good friend Alan came into my office late one fall and asked, "Did you see the latest issue of *Cruising World*? Tania Aebi is doing a lecture tour on the East Coast about *Maiden Voyage*."

The book fascinated me. Her father had given her a choice: go to college or go sailing. He would loan her the money for schooling or for a boat, her option. As a college professor, I found the choice alone was food for thought. How does one *really* get educated for life?

Tania chose the boat. And then her father added the caveat: he expected her to sail around the world by herself, writing and selling articles so she could pay him back. Afterward, she wrote the book. It describes her solo voyage around the world on a 26-foot sloop at age 18.

I had loved the book, partly because of her naïveté, partly because of what happens to her relationship with her parents, mostly because of her courage. After all, I'd opted for college without giving a whole lot of thought to how one really obtains knowledge.

At Tania's pre-departure interview, a reporter asked her, "Why are you doing this?"

"I dunno . . . why not?" she responded off-handedly.

"But aren't you scared?"

"Well, yeah, I guess so."

"What makes you think you can do this?"

"I dunno. A whole lot of other ninnies have already done it. I guess I can do it."

Here was a young woman who'd only been sailing a couple of times and knew virtually nothing about navigation, mechanics, electronics, meteorology, heavy weather, anchoring, or even writing. And she takes off *alone* for a two-year, 27,000-mile trip, to places she'd never even read about, in a boat about the size of a large SUV.

When I had first read it I couldn't put the book down, and had recommended it to Alan. He loved it too.

"I saw the article," I told him. "I'll bet she's really interesting."

Alan responded with his usual excitement, "Let's go hear her."

We live in Colorado so that thought struck me as absurd. First, I considered the source: Alan is an artist in the truest sense of the word. Colorado's Salvador Dali.

It was November. Very cold. Sidewalks covered with a two-day-old sloppy snow. Alan had on his usual sandals, those brown woven sort that look like one is wearing a pair of bread baskets—bread baskets with holes in them where white stockinged toes poked out. Rumpled khaki pants. A short-sleeved madras button-down shirt, mostly faded oranges and reds. I couldn't help noticing that neither collar tab was actually buttoned, so the collar looked like those paper airplanes one makes that never fly. Artists, keen observers of all around them, are oblivious to the elements. Maturity was nowhere in the picture.

But the most noticeable thing about Alan was the bag of cookies invariably carried in his right hand. Chocolate chip, as I recall. And in his left was a partially eaten one he used for emphasis. His "let's go hear her," stated with skinny pale arms flailing about, showered the surroundings with beige crumbs. I'm not sure whether the crumbs or the sandals were making the biggest mess on my office carpet, which had begun the day sort of pebbly-gray.

To a management professor like me, Alan's ideas seemed rather *creative*, to be generous about it. Long on enthusiasm, short on logic. I sighed. With Alan, enthusiasm always ranked higher than reason.

Which brings up the second thing that crossed my mind: convenience. It's not like we could drive thirty minutes, maybe an hour, to catch the presentation. Two thousand miles minimum. Each way.

"Hell," I responded, "I'd only go that far to go sailing, not to hear a lecture." We are professors, so lectures are not exactly what most of us would choose to do with our spare time. I thought my comment would be the end of it.

He never blinked. Just shot out of my office saying simply, "I'll work on it."

Alan knew me well. We'd done lots of baseball, football and late night philosophizing together, not to mention committee meetings. A lecture wasn't going to get my attention. But I am a patsy for an *adventure*—anywhere, anytime, for virtually any lame reason. And an adventure requiring some organizing is a double bonus.

One of the great perks of teaching is the freedom to get away often to all sorts of odd places. In my case, mystery and challenge are expected. "Critical research," I'd always say, and fool no one.

Not a week later Alan is back and says, "Okay, Beau and George are in." Not terribly reassuring actually. Beau had less sailing experience than Tania when she began; and George's behavior was normally as eccentric as Alan's ideas. Good guys but odd bedfellows, I thought.

A close buddy of Alan, Beau has a strong personality. Tall, handsome, good dresser: the kind of guy people notice. Always has great stories and jokes to tell. "Fit in" since the day he was born. Naturally, he took several other guys' trips that were annual events, saltwater fishing and the Daytona 500 among them. Right at home in the spotlight. Confident, gregarious. All those things helped make him a very successful entrepreneur even before he decided to chuck it all and teach. Still, the classroom gave him an audience every day. Mutual love.

George, in contrast, is introspective with large dirty glasses. His office is a library after an earthquake. If you want him to find something, give him half a day's notice and remind him twice. Pink and pudgy. Quirky. Unpredictable. Insufferably brilliant. Growing up, I doubt he *ever* fit in, and he likely took defiant pride in that. An acerbic wit, his humor is lightning quick, though not malicious, unless aimed at some institution or societal norm. I'm not sure his mother liked him (at a minimum, she didn't understand him), but I'm not sure he'd care. I didn't say it to Alan, but I thought one of us would kill him in two, three days. Especially Beau.

In any case, after talking with Alan, and whatever spin he put on my response to the idea, they *expected* to go—even when they knew who'd be there.

So I thought hard about the advice Tania's mother had given her: "Live for the day. Do great things." Going to hear Tania and then sailing wasn't going to qualify as anything great, but I certainly didn't want to be worse than a ninny and do *nothing*. Probably'd be fun too.

So there we were: Flaky, Shaky, Studly and Scout. All a little crazy, all with a thirst for adventure, all looking for escape, for one reason or another. In time we'd find those reasons out.

The next thing you know we four 40-somethings, collectively believing we'd better grab some gusto before we lost our courage along with our hair, were having lunch together looking at everything from timing to locations to boats.

George had extensive sailing experience, Alan and I a fair bit. Beau's principal contribution was knowing South Florida like a good story; and the best venue to see and hear Tania appeared to be Fort Lauderdale in February.

After the predictable banter about whether we were really going to do this, we began working on the details.

I started it off: "I guess I can look for boats. Did a fair bit of chartering when I lived in the islands. I know some sources."

Beau staked his priorities immediately. "Get one with big bunks. Four big bunks."

"That and affordability don't normally come together."

George, who generally spent money before he had it, spoke up. "Affordability matters."

"Not as much as sleep," said Beau, not about to concede.

"Rib-eye mismarked as bologna," I responded. "No problem."

Alan put his oar in the water. "I'll see what I can find on flights to Florida."

"Great," said Beau. "I'll make up a provisioning list and circulate it."

George rarely let a moment for sarcasm pass. "Why? You're gonna ignore our food preferences anyway."

"True," Beau added casually. "But you'll feel you had input. It's my own form of participative decision-making."

"Ah, the illusion of inclusion," I noted. "One of my favorite management concepts. By the way, what are *you* going to do, George?"

"Keep the rest of you afloat."

It turned out Beau had dozens of ideas about what to do before and after the trip, and between Fort Lauderdale and, oh, Marathon, halfway down the Keys. We don't remember that George did anything before we left. But he came on the first two of what were to become ten trips, and he provided us with many of the laughs, not to mention sailing skills. None of us had ever sailed the Keys, though Beau had certainly fished them a lot.

In the end we heard Tania's lecture, sailed, hung out in the Keys, and . . . Ah, but I'm ahead of myself.

1

Florida and the Keys

No man will be a sailor who has contrivance enough to get himself into a jail; for being in a ship is being in a jail, with the chance of being drowned. A man in jail has more room, better food, and commonly better company.

—Samuel Johnson

B eau is 6'6" and a former starter for the Georgia Bulldogs basketball team. A southern gentleman with a Tom Selleck smirk. He owned a cattle ranch for awhile, and he doesn't like cramped spaces. So at the Miami airport he'd arranged for the rental car: clearly the biggest Lincoln ever made. The back seat seemed to be in another zip code. Conversations were east-west across the seats since communicating from front to back was impossible unless the radio was off, which it never was.

Beau found an "oldies" station we all loved. Alan and I, confined to the back seat as the little people, sang along as loud as we could to nearly all of the stuff they played. Free spirits at last. Didn't appear to be much going on in the front seat, though Beau chimed in on a couple of songs. We'd nearly lost our voices by the time we found our destination.

Tania's lecture was in a high school auditorium. Drab, as most of them are, but that night it had the electric air of an America's Cup. Fans awaiting their rock star. We were part of an audience of maybe a hundred mesmerized sailors, all living vicariously through her circumnavigation.

On stage, Tania was dwarfed by a huge projection screen behind her. She had a very firm grip on the podium. Maybe it kept her from blowing away: she looked so small and frail, covered on top by this massive mound of curly brown hair. She was ramrod straight, however; no question who had command of this ship.

Besides her size, though, she was softened by her appearance: pregnant, and clad in a dress that looked to be right out of *Fried Green Tomatoes*, kind of '70s frock. Overall, a contradictory picture.

Tania spoke for maybe an hour, gently and softly, almost inaudibly, accompanied by her slide show. She was amazingly nonchalant about what she'd done and the obstacles she'd overcome.

During the Q&A period, hands flew up all over the place, and one guy asked, "You just taught yourself celestial navigation going from New York to Bermuda?"

Tania responded offhandedly, "Not really much else to do for two weeks."

The questions kept coming. "Wasn't the weather awful?"

She shrugged. "I dunno. A couple of gales hit before Bermuda. Ruined my electronics. No batteries. No radio. I had contaminated water in my tanks. And a leak that nearly sunk me once."

"It seems you also never had a working engine for two years."

"You get pretty good getting in and out of tight places." Her riveting eye contact gave way to a small smile. "Sometimes you row your dinghy and drag the boat."

"What did you do when you were capsized by the tanker in the Med?"

"Well, I guess I got up, dried off and kept going. I had to finish the trip and get home."

What an inspiration! Tania is one incredible sailor. If we needed motivation for our trip, she provided it. She was so unassuming, so *nice*. She just seemed so vulnerable, and she was, let's acknowledge the obvious, a female.

George had to run out during intermission to buy the book as we all wanted our individual copies autographed. The inscriptions all read the same but we didn't care.

If Tania could live her big dream, surely we could live our little one: try not to kill ourselves in the Keys. In spirit, although she didn't know it, Tania was with us from the moment we left the auditorium.

First stop after that was at Papa Joe's Lounge and Restaurant in Islamorada, where we were picking up our boat. Everyone there gave Beau the "long lost brother" routine. Next day's headline might have read, "Basketball Hero and Successful Entrepreneur Returns Home." The subheading might have said, "Accompanied by Three Pale Eating Machines."

We ate seafood as though we were from, well, Colorado. Seafood deprivation. We desperately needed, and got, a fish fix. Grouper. Piles of it, accompanied by coleslaw and side orders of conch fritters. Beer in long-necks that sweated into little pools on the table.

Then we were ready for the marina. The boat was a Pearson 39 with a draft of about 5 feet. It seemed like a good choice at the time, save for the short bunks. We were doing what's called "bare boating," where those who charter are the crew. No professional help aboard. Confident enthusiasm. Not to be confused with competent enthusiasm.

We headed north and we were in heaven. Blue sky, turquoise clear water flying off the bow with a hiss, gigantic white mainsail and jib arced-out taut, palm trees disappearing off the transom, the smell of salt air. Everything we'd dreamed. Had the stereo turned up louder than wives would've allowed.

Being on that boat was like racing in a red Ferrari with the top down. Something else the wives would have discouraged. No lines on the road either.

We did a lot of grinning and smacking each other's shoulders: congratulations all around on our collective wisdom. The only weird part was spreading lotion on another guy's bare back. Actual touching is unavoidable. Women seem to accept that more easily than guys. We did it, but out of duty.

Alan and I had rented air tanks from somewhere in town to scuba dive "Hen and Chickens" on Pennecamp Reef, a national park. But of course it's under water so not readily visible.

"Do we know where to go?" I asked.

Beau responded with his usual confidence, "I know where the reef is."

Alan was unsure. "Yeah, but you don't dive. Fishing is sort of a 'somewhere-in-this-part-of-the-ocean' thing. We gotta be *on* it."

Beau brushed off challenges to his Florida expertise. "I'll get you in the area," he said rather patronizingly. "That's why you've got those tanks, isn't it? So you can explore?"

I felt I had to remind him: "You can't anchor in the park. What are you and George going to do?"

"Go sailing," said Beau.

"That's just great. How are you going to find us in 45 minutes?"

"We'll look for bubbles." Now he sounded cocky.

Oh *sure*, I'm thinking. "Gonna be damn tough to find those little bubbles if you're far off."

"Trust us," George said casually, a smug little smile on his face.

"Why? One of you has never been here; the other can't sail."

But when Alan and I came up, there they were, not fifty meters away, waving at us. We were a bit surprised, *very* relieved.

The sailing was exquisite. Flat water, steady winds. Still able to pick up the oldies station. And we were still singing along at the tops of our lungs. Well, except for George who still seemed to be contemplating whether he'd signed onto the *Ship of Fools.*

Next day we were doing about six knots along the continental shelf, moving too fast for even Beau to fish. Sails perfectly trimmed, boat heeled maybe 15-18°. Suddenly there was a large wake close behind us.

Alan was stunned when he noticed. "Gawd, what's *that*?"

George rather sleepily looked up from reading something, probably a chart. Charts fascinated him. He peered over and volunteered, "Can't be a shark: no fin." He seemed only slightly interested, certainly not concerned.

Now I was into it too, and glanced back from the helm. "It's sure making a helluva big bubble behind the boat."

Alan's eyes were now gigantic, showing a lot of white on what had already become a very red face. "Gotta be *huge.*" I thought he was gonna pull out his sketch pad.

Beau, our acknowledged expert on anything that swims, took a look. "What's huge and brown and going at exactly our speed?"

The speculation went on for several more minutes before we realized we'd snagged a lobster trap on our rudder. Ninnies.

I, not for the last time, tried to be the voice of reason. "Let's slow down and release it." It sounded more like a plea than a suggestion.

George, always on the lookout for a meal, especially a free one, was now *very* interested, and instantaneous in his reaction: "What'ya, nuts? There could be lobsters in there."

"Even if there are, they belong to someone else." It came out more moralistic and preachy than I intended. A frequent problem.

"Do you see anyone around?" Alan added, sounding surprisingly like George. We hadn't seen another boat for over an hour.

Beau shot him a glance. "Have you ever seen *Dead Calm*?"

I made one last effort. "This has gotta be illegal."

Beau remained the authority on all things Floridian. "We're sailing at six knots. We're not even sure where we picked it up. Besides, in the time we've talked about this we're way out of the area where we hooked it."

Alan by now had clearly joined the other two. "No one's looking for us."

"Yet," I added, and conceded defeat.

Consensus was on the side of at least *checking* the trap before releasing it. I suggested we stop to haul it aboard, but Beau assured us he could get it with a boat hook.

George took the helm, and Beau hung over the transom, hook in hand, while Alan and I kept him from becoming one more sea creature, gripping his belt and feet. Hanging onto an ex-basketball player, one large enough to enjoy the body-sacrificing part of that sport and eating enough to put on a few post-college pounds, was *not* easy.

At six knots it took a *long* time to bring that thing in. Beau thrashed around like he was going for a loose ball. Several near man-overboards. All for a potentially empty wood box.

But the trap contained four large greenish-brown lobsters that were scurrying around in there, climbing over each other and pinching the wooden slats. Lots of frantic activity.

"What'ya know," observed George. "Four lobsters, four guys. Nice coincidence." His comments seemed to be aimed in my direction.

Alan was shooting pictures. "No chance these babies are going back now."

Beau smiled. "Good thing we have an ice cold bottle of Chardonnay. Put 'em in a bucket."

"Alright," I said. "I'm as hungry as the rest of you. But don't they remind you just a bit of us? Trapped together in that box with no place to go?"

"Dead right," said George. "They got in there voluntarily. Probably had Tania's book in there too, before we came along. Been in there way too long now. Starting to panic. Like us in a coupla more days. We're saving 'em from killing each other."

They *did* act as though they were happy to be rescued. It was our pleasure.

Sure, it was bad manners or worse; but even if the guilt quotient varied across the group, they made us feel like successful pirates. Our first adventure! They also made for a great cocktail hour when we anchored later that afternoon.

And anchoring was one of our specialties. None of us really knew how far from shore, how far from *anything*, one had to anchor when on the "shelf."

One afternoon we chose a spot, but were unsure whether our depth sounder was measuring from the waterline, the transducer or the keel. And I'm the one who wants to know the anchor is really well dug in: the charter was in my name. So I dove overboard to look.

When I surfaced, Alan asked, "How deep is it?"

"A bit shallow," I replied. "Damned lucky I didn't break my neck." Then stood up. The water was right at my shoulders. We had maybe 6 inches of water under the keel.

That sent the three of them into gales of laughter, mixed with the usual supportive comments.

"You picked a great spot, skipper." ... "Sure hope the tide's out." ... "Want us to pass you a beer?" ... "Good thing you're in charge. Don't want to risk *my* neck." ... "Why don't you just stand out there and *hold* the boat in place?" ... "Wanna come back aboard and dive in again? Maybe you can actually *hit* the anchor."

We had to move.

Sometime between lobster tails and dinner Beau announced, "I don't do dishes."

I was stunned. "Yes, you do. Everyone does dishes. Everyone does everything. We're in this together. Equal shares."

"Not me. I cook, but I don't do dishes."

George was vigorously pursuing the last bit of lobster meat from shell sections the rest of us found decidedly unappealing. But he chimed in, never looking up, "Did you mention this three months ago?" Ever the irreverent colleague, George specialized in having a familiar little *edge* to his contributions.

"Didn't seem relevant." Beau was sipping a rum and tonic. No eye contact.

Alan became the third member of the opposition: "Well, it was and it is. How do we know you can cook?"

"Trust me," said Beau, blowing smoke rings from a very large cigar.

"A line that sounds faintly familiar," I noted. Nothing in the picture would instill trust.

Beau didn't take offense, but he looked just a bit taken aback when he glanced over at me. "I was there when you came up, wasn't I?"

"Yeah, but depending on you for sustenance," said Alan, "that's basic."

"So was saving you two from drowning." Beau refilled his drink from a large plastic pitcher.

There were a few minutes of silence while we all took stock of the fact we had several more days to go and there was no escape. Lobsters.

Finally I blurted out, "Okay, let's try it. You cook every night, and we'll rotate who does the dishes."

"Deal."

What Beau knew and the rest of us did not, was that he can dirty every pot, pan, bowl, utensil, glass and plate in preparing *any* meal. Great meals, sure; but interminable dishwashing sessions. Took all three of us. Every night. We used paper plates the rest of the time.

The next day Alan, Beau and I tried bone fishing in the dinghy. This is a sport normally done in very shallow water from a flat boat pushed by a pole. It helps if the poler is perched high up on a seat so he can see the fish. Dinghies are low. You're blind at water level even with fancy new polarized sunglasses. However, Beau was the only one who even knew what a bone fish was, so he gave instructions and handled the oars.

"There's one," said Beau almost frantically. "Ten yards ahead, moving left to right. Put it right in front of him."

I cast, but replied, "Don't see 'im."

"You missed him," sighed Beau.

"Well I didn't see 'im."

"I didn't either," said Alan. "I think it's your imagination, Beau."

"He was there," Beau assured us. "You just missed him. Gotta be quicker."

"Sounds like your coach at Georgia."

This situation repeated itself a half dozen times with Alan and me alternating on who made the cast. Mostly we just tried to avoid putting a lure into each other's ear. We had no flies, which was just as well since fly casting would have been even more hazardous.

Beau at his basketball height might have helped us spot the fish sooner, but standing up in a dinghy is something only a native Coloradoan would try. Actually, he couldn't have stood up even if he'd wanted to. We were rocking the dinghy and laughing so hard the fish could have heard us. Which might explain why we didn't catch anything.

Speaking of noises, another memorable event on this trip was the discovery that George snores. He snored loud enough to scare off all the bone fish if we hadn't already done so.

It seemed to create a sort of sonic resonance with the hull. Like a thousand foot soldiers running across a wooden bridge. When they all got to the other side, they'd wait a few seconds, then run back across. They did this for *hours*. So after one night we made him sleep in the cockpit.

This snoring machine is housed in a very large pink body covered with freckles—Opie at 5'9" and 210. Relevant because George's other distinctive behavior is nudity. A completely irreverent nude.

What we faced when we came on deck with our morning coffee was a pinkish freckled walrus look-a-like, snoring at foghorn levels. It was almost enough to send us back to bed.

Beau, the southern gentleman, found this unacceptable. After a couple of days he couldn't contain himself, and sneered, "Do you have to sleep naked?"

George was mildly offended. "I always sleep naked. If I wasn't out here you'd never notice."

"But you *are* out here. We all have to look at you."

"Too bad," George responded, without moving.

"Not too bad. Disgusting."

"I never thought so."

"You can't see it. We can."

George rolled over, which didn't help. "Just sleep longer. Maybe I'll dress by then."

"I doubt it."

"Me too."

Good thing he brought plenty of sailing savvy and lots of laughs. Fortunately when we played poker around the table at night most of the worst of it was below sight lines.

After five continuously adventurous days and nights we were back ashore, which was almost as much fun as the sailing. (In Islamorada "Big Dick and The Extruders," the local rock band, didn't *begin* playing until midnight.) The Lincoln carried us north to Beau's former home of Daytona and we felt obligated to conduct a survey on the best tasting conch fritters. The more data points the better. Took us ten hours to cover 250 miles.

Once there we hooked up with two of his buddies who wanted to go *back* to Miami for the boat show. What else we got to do? One of them had a private plane, so we retraced our route, by air, to look at boats we wished, in moments of pure fantasy, we'd chartered. Who'd have thought four guys with PhDs still drooled?

Afterward, we sat down to relax, something at which we'd become expert. Beau was slowly sipping a beer. "Did you see the size of the bunks in that 60-footer?"

Just to remind him we were teachers, I responded, "We couldn't afford to rent the bunks, much less the boat."

"We're trying to live our dreams here," he said, lighting a gigantic cigar.

Alan lit one too, though a smaller one, then thought for a moment. "Some of us dream of stuff other than big beds."

Beau was unoffended. "Big beds help big dreams."

Looking up briefly from a "boats-for-sale" magazine he was

flipping through, George could not seem to stop himself: "Only if you're a giant."

Beau gave him one of those slanty-eyed glances. "Look, we weigh the same. I'm just a foot taller."

"But I fit in a bed."

"How would you know?"

That cracked us up again. Still, we got Tania's message: what matters is not the size of the bed, but the size of the dream.

So rather than dwell on what was truly out of reach, we decided to hit Joe's Stone Crab before flying back. Huge piles of crab legs and ice cold beer. (Happily, the pilot abstained.) That was a dream that took no courage, just an appetite. A capacity none of us ever seem to lack.

Somewhere along the way we discovered we could get along with each other for several days in a confined space without a homicide. All we needed was enough rum, lots of laughter, and a wide variety of cigars. Adventure was essential too. It was the real reason we were there. At least that's what we thought at the time. Maybe it was more basic.

George was able to return to a simpler life for awhile. Alan got out of town for a week. Beau got to hang out with a bunch of guys who hadn't heard his stories, and collect some new ones. And I got a chance to discover.

So we found ourselves discussing the possibility of actually doing this again. Once we recovered.

And recover we did, on the way back to Colorado. Our four wives, no doubt thinking this trip was "the guys' one big fling," met us at the Denver airport in a limo to deliver us all home. We, of course, thought the limo would become the norm. Both wrong.

2

The Caribbean

In certain places, at certain hours, gazing at the sea is dangerous. It is what looking at a woman sometimes is.

—Victor Hugo

A month later we met to exchange photos. We promised we'd all come in cutoffs and Hawaiian shirts. We did, except Beau. Said he forgot but we knew better. I'm not sure what looked more ridiculous: we three dressed, in mid-winter, like we were off to a Jimmy Buffett concert, or Beau sitting there in sharp contrast. Navy blazer, dark gray slacks, starched white shirt with French cuffs, wine-red tie with tiny yellow flowers on it, *considerably* smaller than the ones on our shirts.

George even wore his visor from trip one and he left it on. We'd all bought them in Florida somewhere, then signed each other's since at the time we thought it might be a one-shot deal.

The visors were going to be our party favors. They had a bit more than signatures actually, personalized messages like "Take a cooking class," "Next time bring clothes," "To the bone fishing champ," "Who came up with this stupid idea?" "Helm Hog," "Team Lobster," "Cookie Thief." Stuff like that.

Once we quit playing pool (this restaurant has a great pool room) and sat down to eat, we discovered the first trip had resulted in some sort of epiphany, realizing guy adventures, conversing in guy talk, smoking guy-type cigars, farting without fear, going wherever we damn well felt like. *Loud* music. No morning-after judgments from spouses. No shopping.

The week was short, but intense in a guy sorta way. This

formula *worked*. So even before we got into the pictures we decided on another meeting to discuss the logistics of a repeat.

A month later, same four guys, a year older, looking for new worlds to conquer, new places to go. It was unclear whether Beau or George ever read Tania's book, but it *was* clear we'd all been infected with her "just *go*, life's-no-dress-rehearsal" bug.

In the Keys we had to anchor way too far out to dinghy into the nightlife, which is, of course, essential on a guys' trip since we were trying to live vicariously through guys half our age dancing with girls who look half of theirs. Not to mention their maturing younger than they used to.

The continental shelf sticks out a *long* way. Sharply inhibits ogling. So Florida was out. Consensus on that was reached before the first beer arrived.

The Caribbean seemed to be the logical alternative. We had to escape the Colorado winter, so we needed something warm and exotic, with pure white beaches. Islands. Palm trees. The stuff of men's dreams. Tania was whispering in our ears to push harder, think bolder.

St. Martin/St. Barts was the winner. Islands with French and Dutch cultures, out of the U.S. entirely, gin-clear water. None of us had ever been there, so exploration was still on the priority list. Irresistible allure. Bali Hai practically in our back yard. It was definitely calling us.

We struggled with when to go since there was no lecture to attend. Even harder was deciding how long to stay. The issue was determining the optimum period for four guys to be together before the fish began to smell. How long until the adventure became tedious and we all wished, whether we'd admit it or not, for the company of our wives? We had different responses to that question.

"I'll go for as long as I can get away," offered George. "Ten days, two weeks."

"Me too," I added. "The longer I'm sailing the better I like it."

Alan's face was completely passive. "If I'm gone more than a week, including travel, I may as well not go home. There'd be new locks." Alan's "escape need" had to be met with intensity, not duration.

"That's five days on the boat," said Beau. "I can't stand you

guys longer than that anyway. Might risk screwing up the friendships."

"Hell, you're just worried you might run out of stories," I said.
"You wouldn't have anything to talk about."

"Never a problem. A couple of rum and tonics gives me total
recall. But friendships can be fragile on a boat."

"Doesn't matter," said George. "None of us like you anyway. We
just needed someone to show us around Florida. Going to the
Caribbean, you're expendable."

Beau didn't even look up from studying his day-timer. "Not if
you want any decent meals."

Of course we *did*, since eating well was an essential ingredient of
our formula. No one wanted a hostile cook. So we settled on five
days in February. After that the details fell right into place. And
when the time to depart grew near, we became almost giddy. Buffett
tapes got a lot of airtime. To and from work, in the car, I sang along.
Really loud.

The first of our new island experiences came before we ever got
off the plane. George and I arrived on St. Martin late one night in a
heavy rainstorm. Niagara Falls. Scary, really. The DC-10 came to the
end of the runway, then gently slid just far enough beyond to bury
its nose wheel in the mud. Serious mud. Took one of those airport
plane movers two hours to extricate us.

Hot as hell in that cabin even at midnight, and no free drinks.
Sticky. After about an hour it began to smell a bit too tropical. The
locker room after a 1 p.m. game in August. Some of the nearby conversation seemed downright hostile. George and I found it amusing.

"What do you think," he asked, "about having open windows
on all planes flying south?"

"Maybe a bit impractical," I responded. "But open bars would
be nice."

No question those around us would've agreed.

We got off the plane into the heaviest air I've ever felt. And the
hubbub of island life. The biggest problem thereafter was getting
everyone to the same place. George and I (the only two there) took
the Kirie 42 out of St. Martin's Simpson Bay Lagoon in the dark since
in those days the drawbridge only opened twice a day, the first at 6

a.m. No hint of the sun, but we had to get that mast past the bridge and into open water if we wanted to go anywhere.

"Damn, this lagoon is crowded," I said. "Boats and buoys everywhere. I can't see anything 'till we're right next to it." We were motoring away from the marina, out toward the bridge. Both standing in the cockpit. I was at the helm; George was sweeping the water with a flashlight.

"Lots of liveaboards," responded George. "Though none of 'em up yet."

"If we hit one we'll fix that in a hurry."

"I'll go out on the bow."

He yelled back instructions at a volume that would have made a collision redundant. Anyone in the neighborhood was up. Good thing he was dressed.

We anchored just beyond the bridge and spent the morning dinghying to a nearby hotel to find out what happened to the other two guys. Our university's voicemail system was the only means of communication. Leave a message and hope the other guy picks it up; then go back in a couple of hours and hope he's left one in return. Uncertain. Slow. Damned inconvenient in the days before cell phones. Island telephone "service" didn't help.

Beau was supposed to have been with us, but he missed the plane in Denver. Alan had been called out of state at the last minute on a family emergency. So George and I were on a very large yacht with no idea if or when we'd have additional crew.

Five hours and a hundred dollars worth of international phone calls later, not to mention a relationship with the local phone operator that would have threatened, had it existed, the North American Free Trade Agreement (is this how wars start?), we determined Beau was, so he said, coming in that afternoon, Alan a day later.

We were sitting in the cockpit, halfheartedly playing blackjack, using matchsticks for money, as usual. Mostly we were nursing a couple of beers, making sure they stayed in the shade. Eating potato chips. Guy meal.

"Okay," I said. I was consciously waving a chip around, trying to imitate Alan and his cookies. But I didn't have Alan's artistry; George didn't notice. "Let's summarize. We think Beau's coming in this afternoon at 3:00, assuming he actually made his connection in San Juan, didn't get off to go gambling, and that his flight's on time."

"That's about it," George responded. "Mostly guesswork. Like this hand. Better hit me."

"Queen. You're busted. Maybe we should've ordered a boat phone."

"No chance," George said dismissively. "We came to escape."

"We've certainly done that," I said. "No one knows where we are, including the other two guys."

"Reduces the whining by 50%."

"And the decent meals by 100%, unless you count cookies as all four food groups."

"I take back what I said about whine reduction, Tom. You're making up for the other two."

We fell silent for several minutes, sipping occasionally. George was shuffling the cards indifferently. I sighed, "Looks like it's our job to find *them*. Let's list our options."

"We could just take off. Forget 'em." offered George. There was just a kernel of sincerity in his voice. "They can't be here on time, to hell with 'em."

"Intriguing," I said facetiously, "but I couldn't stand that much snoring and nudity alone. Too big a burden."

"Just kidding anyway," he grunted. "In some perverse way, I'd miss 'em."

"Funny. Perverse is a word I once heard attached to *you*."

He ignored me and dealt. "One thing's certain. The bridge isn't going back up until 6:00 tonight, so we're not taking this boat over to get Beau." The airport was across the lagoon. He seemed to get increasingly reflective as he sunk lower and lower on the cockpit seat. "It's a big island. Walking is out. Besides, we'd have to leave our dinghy tied up on some beach. It could disappear."

"Hell, *we* could disappear. A coupla continentals like us'd get lost in five minutes. Think a cab might stop?"

"Doubt it."

"Me too." Several more minutes passed. We silently played a few more hands, exchanging a few more matchsticks.

"You up for a dinghy ride?" I asked.

"Helluva long way. Two miles to the airport, I'd say. Gonna take an hour. Major problem if the motor quits."

"Even worse if we get there and Beau doesn't."

We batted it around for awhile longer, never coming up with a decent alternative. In the end it seemed the only reasonable way to retrieve Beau was to take the dinghy under the bridge and traverse the couple of miles downwind across the lagoon to the airport. Tie up, find him—if he was there—and head back. No problem. Assuming the dinghy motor held out.

We barely caught him just as he was jumping into a cab. We don't know where he was headed because he had no idea where we'd anchored the yacht. But the *taxi driver* had convinced Beau he could find us. Right.

We told Beau he owed us $100 for saving him from an endless tour of the island. He'd still be there, roaming around, peering out his window, looking for a boat he couldn't identify, cooped up in a small space with some tropical guy he didn't know who wouldn't even listen to his stories. Beau would have been suicidal. Or homicidal. Good thing we needed a cook.

The return trip to the yacht was eventful. Beau had two very heavy bags, he's large, and we ended up with about 4 inches of freeboard on the dinghy.

Beau was very happy to see us, of course, but less happy about the conveyance. "This is the smallest dinghy I've ever seen."

"It's what they gave us," I said.

"You should have asked for something bigger," he chastised. "They don't know how big I am. George fills this thing up all by himself."

George never flinched. "Don't start. Could be a long week."

"I *did* ask," I said. "It's all they had at the marina."

Beau was getting wetter and madder by the minute. He was clearly 24 hours behind George and me getting into an adventurous spirit. "Let's go over there," he demanded. "I'll talk to them."

We were both barefoot, in cutoffs and T-shirts, thinking this was pretty hilarious. We glanced at each other, laughed, then looked right at him. "Forget it. Just bail."

Against the wind the dinghy took on so much water we had to

bail like hell to keep from sinking. And we had only our hands and two empty beer cans. We were drenched almost immediately. Not that it mattered to two of us.

Everything Beau brought was soaked by the time we reached the yacht. Wet clothes, especially for George, were a new experience. But rum has a warming effect. Unfortunately the cigars were a casualty of the dinghy ride.

Cigars had already become one of our rituals. We were determined to find, no matter how long the research took, the finest hand rolled, flavorful, not-too-fat, not-too-long, not-too-strong cigar on the market. For $2 or less. Professors are notoriously cheap. We just wanted to *look* wealthy.

The first year we'd all brought some. Needed lots of data for proper research. Since none of us smoke except on self-proclaimed special occasions, the selection, well, stunk.

So for year two, Beau, who had at least tried several kinds on his other guys' outings, brought them all. Nice selection, wide variety of shapes and strengths. An improvement over randomness. Obviously it was a crisis when on one memorable dinghy ride, they all became hopelessly saturated.

As soon as we got Beau aboard the yacht, George and I dinghied back to the hotel to make one more phone call: to Alan to stock up on whatever cigars he could find on short notice. (Beau refused to go since he was temporarily clad in George's clothes, who didn't need them, all of which were about 4 inches too short. No chance of a public appearance.) That night, alas, we did without cigars. But it was the *only* time.

Finally got moving the following morning. Winds hit 25 knots and we *flew*. Thought about going all the way up to Grande Case but it was too far from the airport and Alan's arrival. So we just sailed around for hours having a blast. We got wet again; this time all of us loved it. We dropped the anchor in Marigot Bay.

Marigot is big, maybe the size of Rhode Island. Okay, maybe twenty football fields. It was almost totally empty. A hundred meters to our nearest neighbor.

We were hanging out for an hour or so, enjoying our first rum and tonic of the day, when another yacht came in and anchored *right next to* us. It was flying a foreign flag that shall go unidentified. (But

the same three colors as ours. One stripe each. Wide.) We could practically shake hands. If we'd wanted to.

"Do you have to anchor right there? There's plenty of room." I
didn't have to shout: he was really close.

The skipper assured us, in a mixture of English and his native
tongue, that he was very competent and our boats would not touch
if they swung. Lots of hand gestures.

"Not our point actually," I said. "This is an enormous anchorage. We'd like to have dinner alone."

Didn't phase him, so we pulled out our secret weapon. George
emerged from down below in his favorite outfit. Buff. Took that boat
less than five minutes to haul anchor and move. A *long* way off.

"Okay, George," noted Beau, gesturing with his glass. "You're
good for something after all."

After dinner that evening Beau offered to take a cab to meet
Alan at the airport. When all four guys were finally together aboard
the boat we stayed awake way too long catching up. Next day we
sailed for St. Barts.

I thought Alan looked a little green around the gills when he
emerged. "Want the helm? It might make you feel better."

He was apparently immobile. "Nothing could make me feel
better—except talking softer."

"C'mon. We didn't drink that much."

"Maybe you didn't. I don't remember."

Now I felt sorry for him. A little. "Why don't you go back to
bed? George is on the sails. Beau wants to fish. You're useless
anyway."

"Can't stand being down below," he responded, barely moving
his lips.

"Well, I don't want you too close to me while we're bouncing
around."

"Even *I* don't want to be too close to me."

Alan spent nearly that whole day lying prone on the leeward
rail (dangerous for him, sure, but safer for us) with a death grip on
the lifeline stanchions. Every once in awhile the lee rail would dip in
the ocean and he'd get soaked. But he never moved. He seemed to
be concentrating on orally creating a new type of colorful painting
on the water. Remarkable, the inventiveness of artists.

Our anchorage that night was in gorgeous Colombier Bay. It looks directly west, high hills form the other three sides. Since the sky was absolutely clear, we thought we had a shot at seeing the green flash. This is a meteorological phenomenon that occurs only under perfect conditions. Just as the last bit of sun disappears, in the instant of its vanishing, a thin, bright green flash shoots across the horizon. Blink and you miss it. I'd spent a year living on St. Thomas, never seeing it once. That night, for the first and last time, we saw it. *Fast*. Glorious. Unforgettable.

Colombier is a great place for lots of other things too, including snorkeling and hiking on shore. We even tried windsurfing, since we had a board with us. Only George was able to tack; so when the rest of us tried it we kept one guy in the dinghy to rescue the boarder when he got too far downwind. And too tired to move, after climbing, time after countless time, back onto that board. George's lessons failed to improve the skill levels of the rest of us.

It's important to note here that Alan, a happily married man, has a normal artist's fascination with form, in this case the female form. St. Barts is French. The Caribbean French, at least in Colombier Bay, hang out nude. Totally.

George was right at home. Alan was a diabetic in a candy store. He examined French women, even on yachts maybe 50 feet away, with binoculars, and even though he usually had to put down a cookie to hold them.

"Is that really necessary?" I asked. "Those people are practically in our laps."

Alan never looked up: "Wow."

Our southern crewmember was also offended. "It's really rude, Alan. Glance and look away."

Alan, adjusting the focus from boat to boat: "Incredible."

It appeared the binoculars were permanently affixed to his face. I took another stab. "It's worse than rude. It's embarrassing."

But he responded, "Not to me."

"It's pretty obvious we're Americans," Beau said.

Alan was not conceding anything. "It was pretty obvious anyway."

"Not *this* obvious," I remarked.

"If they didn't want us to look, they'd put on clothes."

"It's cultural, Alan. They don't wear clothes on this beach."

His eyes never left the glasses. "I can't believe this. Incredible."

I gave it one last shot: "Really, *you're* the one who's incredible." Didn't faze him.

"Unbelievable."

"What?" asked George.

A couple of days later George had to fly back from St. Barts but couldn't find his money to buy the ticket. To this day he believes Beau hid it on the boat; we think he spent it in a bar. The true story will never be known.

We dropped George ashore with his handful of credit cards, but he couldn't get a cash advance. His irreverence for virtually everything, including, maybe especially, financial institutions, caused him to max them out and ignore the bills.

He became just one more freeloader trying to panhandle airfare, albeit a pink, freckled freeloader with a doctorate. He never spoke much about it, and we never asked him anything directly. Beau and he didn't seem to be talking much when we first got home; Alan and

I didn't want to embarrass him, not that we normally refrained from that.

The three who remained aboard returned the boat to St. Martin. We immediately missed George's irreverent humor, his sense of freedom. But it didn't take long to appreciate quiet during the nights.

During one of them we got to talking about why this was so much fun, why we felt so good. We'd become hedonists for a week, if harmless ones. But it wasn't so much the pleasure-seeking. It was, we decided, the complete absence of guilt.

There was simply no guilt about just being guys: smoking cigars, drinking, over-drinking, belching, laughing at dirty jokes. And none about missing a deadline, or a meeting. No guilt about not shaving, not communicating, loud music, being from Mars or having middle-aged body shapes. No guilt period.

Men never really grow up at least with each other. Without a career, kids, or utility bills, most guys never age past twenty. Lots of reflection led us to believe that was a universal truth. The trick was to perfect the art of temporary regression.

We thought it was likely George had experienced this sense of freedom before. He was that kind of guy. But for the three of us, at least, it was cathartic.

We spent a couple of days of R&R in Florida where we took in the Daytona 500, tickets having been secured by our native crewmember. Caution flags during the race made it last so long we almost missed our flight back to Denver. Still, it was the perfect end to a nearly perfect trip. And we were on a roll.

If only there'd been a limo at the airport.

3

St. Martin and St. Barts

The sea finds out everything you did wrong.
—Francis Stokes

Beau, Alan and I wanted a three-peat: the first two years had been a blast. We'd all become fast friends. But George merely said, "I don't think so," and dismissed it. Perhaps he just felt abandoned back on St. Barts. Or broke and didn't want to admit it. Maybe he *needed* it less than the rest of us.

We had a fair bit of ambivalence about his decision. Would this idea end? George was a *part* of it after all, a charter member. He was funny, easy-going, skilled and weird.

Yet in the backs of our heads maybe we relaxed a little, worried that at some point he'd do something totally nuts, ending up drowned or in jail or something. We three thought of ourselves, in contrast, as being more conventional. A bit crazy perhaps, but mainstream crazy: the types that know our mothers are proud of us—so long as we spare them, since birth, the details.

Though George didn't sign on again, he didn't seem to resent our planning another trip either. "You'll find somebody. Go and have fun. Smoke one for me." Six months later he quit the university and just disappeared. He's out there somewhere (literally), but we never heard from him again. Perhaps he alone truly had Tania's wanderlust.

Without him we needed another guy's guy who could immediately fit in, like a rookie who's a flat-out starter. "Fit" was critical: year three had to be even better than one and two. The bar was really up there.

Luckily we found Oz. Not the wizard of course, but a sports

obsessed professor who can make theoretical mathematics fun for even the numerically challenged. True, "fun" and "math" are not often found in the same sentence, but Oz belongs to a very exclusive fraternity. Plus we all liked him.

He shares with George a large, soft-looking frame that is sometimes rumpled, but that's where the resemblance ends. Oz scores high on the warm-and-fuzzy scale, good family man, considerate. More like a social worker than a mathematician. Smiles a lot, even at strangers. What hair he has is prematurely gray. Made him look like the crew's token senior citizen. Well, made us look younger. Surprisingly good tennis player, considering his full figure.

Oz sees humor in everything (clearly one couldn't survive these trips without that), though never at someone else's expense. He brought a softness to the group we'd not had; and he came fully clothed. Sure, he could open a pop top and he loved poker. But he liked it best when nobody lost much.

We were certain he could hold his own in guy talks (which as everyone knows are, on weekends, 75% about sports and 25% about women; 25% sports, 75% women the other days). He smoked the occasional cigar and, like the rest of us, could lie about his past. At least when it came to the two principal subjects of conversation.

Lying about achievements related to sports and women was an essential ingredient. So was the unspoken rule not to say *any*thing about the trip to a non-member when we returned. Especially a female.

We regaled Oz with stories about the first two trips, embellishing only when absolutely necessary; and we convinced him of his need to experience a new sport.

Equally important was a guy willing to bring his share of the limes. By this time we'd discovered we needed to bring our own limes if we wanted really juicy ones.

When told of this, Oz asked, "Why would you carry limes to the islands? It's the tropics, for Pete's sake. They grow 'em there and ship 'em here. We're gonna carry them back?"

"Right," I said. "They've only got *key* limes there. They make great pie of course, but those golf ball-sized nuggets are way short on juice. Besides, we don't want any scurvy aboard." (None of us ever contracted it.)

"Still seems crazy," he responded.

"Well, *we're* crazy," I said. "Ya gotta trust us."

"I don't drink rum and tonics," he added as his final effort at protest.

"You will."

One more little known fact: limes will last all week if you wrap them in tin foil. No late week scurvy.

We told Oz the only other prerequisite for joining was reading *Don't Stop the Carnival*. We think Herman Wouk's novel is a requirement for buying a ticket to the islands. If it's not, it should be. Norman Paperman, the hero, shares a couple of traits with Tania Aebi: courage and naïveté.

Carnival makes it possible for a continental to kick back and take the Caribbean on its own terms: its politics, values, norms, and systems. Sure it's fiction; but you can't get a better introduction to island culture than in the several hours it takes to digest, and laugh through, this book. I'd read it twice when living on St. Thomas, and several times since. Alan and Beau both loved it. Written almost forty years ago. Just as insightful as ever. It's so good Buffett wrote songs for it and turned it into a musical.

Once he'd read *Carnival*, Oz was invited to our next "trip meeting"—events which had become institutionalized: lunches or late afternoon get-togethers where we spread out all the books and charts we'd accumulated. After we'd shot a few games of pool and downed an adult beverage or two. Then began lengthy but friendly debates.

I had become a coordinator of sorts, although *camp counselor* is closer to the reality. "Okay. When can we go?"

Oz immediately announced to the group, "I gotta go during a school break. December or March." No freshman senator silence in this group.

"Why?" Alan asked. "Aren't you team teaching? Get someone to cover for you."

Oz looked at him. "Okay, maybe I can manage that, but what about you?"

"No one would notice he was missing," observed Beau. Clearly we were hitting our old form.

Alan rose to the occasion and blurted, "Easy for you to say since you're never in the classroom these days."

Beau was unoffended. "University administration is hell."

"I never thought so," I said.

Beau peered out through his eyebrows. "You never asked the people working for you."

"Yeah, I did. That's why I went back to teaching."

Oz looked very uncomfortable, not accustomed to this yet. His eyes had been jumping back and forth between us, like he was watching a tennis match. He plunged back in, seeking to diffuse what he thought was an approaching grenade. "We're losing sight of the topic here. Whenever it is, are we assuming a week?"

"Tops," said Beau. "I can't stand being cramped up with a bunch of guys for more than five days. Last year didn't change my mind on *that* issue."

Alan, making up for the absence of George, commented, "Probably because you take up so much space."

"Your wife's not gonna let you be gone for more than that anyway," Beau fired back.

Now Oz was beginning to look mildly concerned. "How small *are* these boats?" He'd never been on a sailboat.

"Some days they seem *real* small," I said. "Especially toward the end of the trip. Picture four lobsters in a small box . . . I'll see if I can get a charter for less than a week."

"Let's try to make February work," offered Alan, who seemed to be off of Beau and onto the topic. "Colorado's miserable in February." Obviously a non-skiing California transplant.

Eventually we got timing out of the way and turned our attention to location. The Caribbean was a given: right temperature, exotic locations. But on this topic all we had were brochure pictures: isolated anchorages, beautiful islands, even more beautiful women. Alan could describe their freckles.

I argued for someplace new, but in the end we concluded we'd not seen enough of St. Martin and decided to go back. Or maybe our thirst for a new adventure temporarily failed us. ("Where's the exploration in a re-run?" I asked. They ignored me.)

But St. Martin is a wonderful place: gambling on the Dutch side, great French food on the other. Perfumy air, bright colors. Terrific selection of boats. Hadn't seen it all the first time, that's for sure. We got Oz pretty fired up.

Returning to a place we had actually visited let us turn more of our conversation to subjects we were good at (cigars, port to go with the cigars, poker paraphernalia, restaurants) and avoid those about which we'd otherwise know little: winds, anchorages, other small stuff.

Ever the connoisseur, Beau wanted to know, "Who's bringing the port?"

Alan brightened and volunteered. "I'll do it. Good vintage this time."

"That's what you said last year," said Beau derisively. "Spend some money. Sell a painting, you cheap ar-teest. Get twenty-year-old stuff. Gotta be worthy of the cigars I'll bring."

"If you could keep 'em dry," retorted Alan.

I was more worried about the food. "What about this provisioning list?"

"I'll do it when I arrive," said Beau. "I do all the cooking anyway."

"Omit the peas this time. I don't like peas," I stated firmly.

"Got a new way to fix 'em."

"Won't help. Nothing you can do to peas makes 'em pleasant. I'm on vacation."

Alan handed Beau a pen so he'd make a note. "More cookies this time. We ran out."

"Maybe because someone ate more than his share," Beau offered.

"Simple solution: you eat Tom's peas; I'll eat your share of the cookies."

Oz didn't want to be left behind. "Whad'ya want me to bring?"

I gave my lime sermon another run. "Limes. Big limes. As many as you can fit in your bag. Wrap 'em in tin foil." The other two nodded.

"Won't that set off the X-ray in the airport?"

"Sure. That's why having 'em all in one bag is better. Everyone else sails through. Make up a scurvy story."

Oz made it through Denver security without incident, along with Alan and me. While we three were waiting in St. Martin for Beau to show up (university administration is hell?), we took the commuter flight to Saba. If you've never landed on this strip-carved-out-of-the-side-of-a-sheer-cliff on Saba, well, add it to your "Everest list." Even Lindbergh would have had white knuckles.

Alan and I went scuba diving again, this time with a local guide. The reef he took us to began at 80 feet and went down from there. It's so dark at that depth we could barely see each other. The fish, wisely, were sunning themselves elsewhere. Our tanks held out just long enough to get us down and back up. Exploration would have to wait.

After "diving Saba" (hell, the bottom is 120 feet down; maybe that *is* hell), we returned to St. Martin to gamble a bit, then pick up the boat, this time a Kirie 46. The three of us sailed around to Orient Bay for our rendezvous with Beau.

He wasn't hard to find the next day since Orient is totally nude and Beau was totally dressed, carrying his luggage. 6'6" and looking very GQ: vertically striped shirt, white shorts, docksiders, big panama hat.

"Great seeing you guys," Beau smiled. "Wasn't sure what I'd do if you didn't show up."

"You weren't hard to spot," I said. "We saw you coming a half mile down the beach."

"Not many guys out here my height," he responded.

"Actually," I noted, "you look odder on that beach dressed than George looked in the buff."

"Odder, perhaps. Certainly prettier. I'll take it as a compliment."

The following morning we had the pleasure of watching the cabana girls put their umbrellas in the sand. It was hard to leave. But we wanted to check out the little island of Tintamarre. After that the idea of a "cheeseburger in paradise" on St. Barts was compelling, so we sailed the fifteen or so miles over.

We noticed something we seemed to have missed before: islands are so much different when approached from the sea. They rise up like black rocks on the horizon, when the sun is shining. A gray outline when it's not. Only as the distance diminishes do the deep greens emerge. Then the white sides of the houses, and soon thereafter their red roofs. And finally, the cars and people—sure signs that the place is populated after all. But it sneaks up on the sailor in a way very unlike the sudden descent into bedlam when arriving by plane. Gentler. Like you're becoming a part of it rather than just visiting. Much more satisfying.

That's how I knew the arrival into St. Barts would be the right moment: maybe it was part of my camp counselor image, but I felt we needed a new feature added to our trips: crew shirts. We wanted to look non-professorial when ashore and I thought the shirts would help.

So I designed a logo: a yacht under spinnaker against a mountain background. Really cool, if I do say so. A friend made up four identical (except for the sizes of course, there being large variations among us) teal polo shirts with this great logo embroidered on the left breast in purple, white and gold. I presented them with a flourish one night on the boat. The guys loved them.

Wore them ashore for the first time in Gustavia, and headed straight for "Cheeseburger." It's a funky looking place: beer-stained dirt floors, green umbrellas over the tables, strings of lights crisscrossing overhead, potted plants in the corners. Large dark bar, stocked like the one we assume is in heaven. The distinct odor of marijuana mixed with the smoke of cigars and cigarettes. We grinned, but the appeal was twenty years old.

We plopped down and ordered beers. The two couples at the table next to us were speaking American. They must have overheard us too. One of the men leaned back and asked, "Where ya from?"

Beau, his basketball reflexes still quick, said, "Lauderdale. You?"

"Indianapolis. Our first charter in the Caribbean."

"Having a good time?"

"Incredible. We couldn't help noticing your shirts."

By now all four of us were into it: "Crew shirts. We just finished the Heineken." (Everything we knew about the Heineken Regatta we'd read in the airline magazine on the way down. It had been that month, at least.)

"No kidding?" The two wives turned back to each other and began talking about something else.

We kept right on rolling. "Yeah. Lotta fun. 200 entries. Great races. Even better parties."

"You guys pros?"

"Nah. We crew for expenses. Alan's a lawyer, Oz here's a psychologist, Beau's an investment advisor, I own a pharmacy."

"Fantastic. You do this often?"

"Maybe 5-6 times a year. Beats staying home." The wives looked ready to leave.

But the Indy guys were captivated. "No joke. What d'ya sail?"

"J-120. Great boat."

"How d'ya do?"

Group chatter: "Second in class. Fourth overall." ... "Yeah, but we busted a halyard in race two." ... "And how 'bout the crappy spinnaker set in four?" . . . "Well whose fault was *that*?" . . . "I think it was the skipper's: he's not here." . . . "He's also the one responsible for banning beer from the boat so we're cuttin' him no slack." . . . "We're here making up for lost time."

"Good life you guys got."

"Yeah, if you don't faint. The pace is a bitch." It began to appear the wives actually resented the shirts.

However, we thought the scam worked so well we had new crew shirts on every trip after that. (Kept the same logo though, of course.) The repartee got very sophisticated. We loved the shirts; but we must have lost our credibility somewhere along the line: people quit asking us about them.

The yacht had been anchored in Gustavia Harbor and we thought we'd top off the water before going anywhere. So we brought her in, swung around beautifully to the gas dock in front of the usual dozen or so spectators. *Stylish.*

Oz, wanting badly to be a full-fledged crewmember, stepped onto the dock with a line. A large puff of offshore breeze hit just as he bent over to cleat the line and he was smoothly but rather quickly pulled into the bay. Surfaced immediately. No harm done.

"Tennis reflexes slowed a bit?" asked Beau, tossing him a loose cushion.

"Miscalculated the odds," suggested Alan, trying to make a math joke and already shooting pictures.

Oz climbed aboard the swim platform. I looked at him sympathetically. "You might want to let that line slip through your hands a bit so you can get a wrap, stay dry."

"In my class," said Oz, "I give the information *before* the test." But he was smiling, as he always was.

Next day was one of the true highlights of this trip: our spinnaker experience. We'd never had one on board before, which could have been a matter of trust with the charter companies. None of us had ever flown one.

"You actually gonna get that thing out?" asked Beau. He was at the helm doing his best to look like Ted Turner.

"Damn right," I said. "Took a class once."

"Now that's reassuring." Had that Turner jauntiness in his voice.

"Okay, the boat was a bit smaller than this, but otherwise no difference."

Alan looked skeptical. "Didn't you have a few more guys and an instructor?"

"Sure," I snapped. "Great teacher, not that you guys would understand. I graduated and I'm ready. Can't have a spinnaker aboard and not fly it."

"What's a spinnaker?" asked Oz.

"It's remotely possible," said Beau, "very remotely, you're about to find out. Meantime, get a good grip on something solid."

"All bullshit," I fired back. "It's a gorgeous thing. You're gonna die when you see it."

"Careful, Oz," Beau noted. "He may be speaking literally."

It took us an hour to get ready (didn't want any mistakes), but it went up perfectly. When it filled, it was *huge.* A gigantic, triangular parachute. And it was beautiful. Pale blue, with lemon, white and royal blue stripes on a diagonal toward the top.

It was *so* beautiful we just had to have a picture of the boat with the chute up. Every sailor's pictorial fantasy. Blow that photo up to about 20x30 and hang it in your office. An eat-your-heart-out conversation starter. "That's us last year," you'd say casually.

So I got in the dinghy with my camera and cast off, somehow not giving much thought to whether the dinghy could keep up with a spinnakered yacht, not to mention the difficulty of running the dinghy wide open while trying to take pictures. They all came out lousy. Plus the crew had to turn the boat upwind and collapse the chute or I'd have become very lonely out there.

Climbing back aboard I observed, "Maybe one of the dumbest things I've ever done."

Oz was sympathetic. "A truly noble gesture."

"Nobility drowns as fast as stupidity."

"Noble nonetheless." It was great to have him along.

We bagged up the spinnaker, got the genoa reset and headed back to St. Barts. Turned out Oz had recently watched a video on Tai Chi for Elders. He gave instructions on our way back in. Between sipping rum and tonics we tried looking graceful without falling overboard. Enthusiasm outweighed grace. We had no trouble looking elderly.

Anchored again in Colombier because we wanted to walk over

to Anse des Flamands. This hike passes through all sorts of incredible vegetation. Huge breadfruit and papaya trees, and smaller ones with guava, tamarind and passion fruit. Cactus, century plants, hibiscus, and bougainvillea are everywhere, all with a breath-taking ocean view all along the way on your left side.

It's only a couple of miles to a tiny little resort on a very secluded beach. Very up-market. Exclusive carries a high price: a beer at the beach bar was $9.50. And you'd better tip.

We decided to return to the yacht where the beer was free. Besides, we were in our favorite anchorage, even without the green flash. Alan couldn't wait to get back. The beach viewing was still spectacularly unencumbered; but we hid the binoculars.

It was on this trip that Alan first brought along a book called *If . . . Questions for the Game of Life* by Evelyn McFarlane and James Saywell. It's full of wonderfully thoughtful questions like, "If you could change the results of one election in history so that the loser had won, which one would it be?" And, "If you were marooned on an island with only one book, which book would it be?" Or, "If you could hire one architect from history to design your dream home, who would you pick and where in the world would you build it?" "If you could have fathered one person in history, who would it have been?" Maybe 500 questions, all thought-provoking.

We gave the book to someone who, without looking, opened to a page, pointed to a question, and asked it. We all had to answer. Then we passed the book to the next guy. Each question could take twenty minutes or so, so we played a couple of rounds after poker most nights. The first night the game went on for hours.

If became a staple on all our trips after that. More than any other single thing, it helped us learn about each other. If Tania was the catalyst to go and live together for a week, this book provided the home in which four guys became genuine friends.

Beyond the book, the entire trip thing had become an annual ritual, not to be tampered with in any real sense. Discussions that night in Colombier and in the weeks to follow focused no longer on whether we would do it again, merely on when and where. (Our wives had either resigned themselves or relished our absence, we're not sure which. Both probably.) But we were determined to recapture Tania's spirit of adventure and head for new horizons. So we did.

4

Guadeloupe

The lovely thing about cruising is that planning usually turns out to be of little use.

—Dom Degnon

We had our usual post-trip meeting, which sort of blended into our pre-trip meetings. We'd become increasingly flexible on when we'd go sailing since the *going* part was a done deal. The big topic this year was where.

A return to the Caribbean was pretty much a given since it offered everything a quartet of Colorado guys needs in the middle of winter. Warmth. Seafood. Great scenery, human and otherwise.

Beyond that we were sick of trying to find a sloop that would allow four guys to sleep privately and in peace. We jumped onto the idea of chartering a catamaran. And we jumped to the island of Guadeloupe, mostly because none of us had ever been there. And it was French. Totally French. Tania was whispering loudly in our ear that year.

Alan was temporarily unavailable so Beau, Oz and I had a quick chat about whom to invite as a fourth. Oz immediately said, "Anyone you guys want is fine with me." We knew that to be not just dismissive, but a true statement. Oz's motivation from the beginning was to hang out, have some fun, and get to know other guys better. A sailing adventure was a means, not an end.

Beau and I decided to approach Darren, who would be our first non-professor. We knew him through mutual acquaintances. He's a banker by profession, which meant that most people found him about as boring as a professor. Good fit. Still, he was outside our newly created "collegial community of sailors."

We knew nothing about Darren's feelings regarding ocean-type stuff, so Beau suggested we sneak up on the topic, maybe during a round of golf. Darren was an especially lousy golfer, but he loved being outdoors and he enjoyed traveling to new places, doing new things. We were optimistic.

We waited until the back nine after we'd exhausted the usual catch-up talk. Following one of Darren's particularly ugly chip shots, Beau commented, "Darren, not to put too fine a point on it, but your game's in the dumper." (Beau is a 6-handicapper, of course.) "You ever thought about sailing?"

"Never. We live in Colorado. No salt water within three states. I don't even like the fact that at my age I've been reduced to golf, but at least I'm on dirt." Immediately he'd displayed the right conversational tone.

I jumped in. "Sure. We all live here because it's heaven; but getting out on the ocean's an incredible experience."

"No doubt. No doubt too there's big waves and sharks."

"We've never seen either," I said; but I glanced at Beau and I knew we were both recalling our initial reactions to the lobster trap and the sleigh ride off St. Martin in 25 knots. We grinned: good thing Darren wasn't there.

Darren executed another pitiful shot. "Then why go?"

This presented a situation in which Beau excels: charm, persuasion, guy-type BS. "To be with a bunch of guys, a thousand miles from everything familiar. Seeing new places—beaches, restaurants, bars, palm trees, naked women. Doing guy things. Playing poker. Yukking it up. We've been going for three years. It's a blast. Never had better times. We're a guy short this year."

"Who do you get to run the boat?" He kept taking practice swings. As though that would help.

"No one," I said. "We're the whole crew. Rotate skippering duties."

"You're short more than a guy," Darren observed. "More like a card short of a deck. It's stupid. You could sink. Drown, even."

But only a couple of shots later he added, "I'll think about it." It sounded like Beau and I were applying for a loan. Still, we could tell he really *was* thinking about it, looking for a few new horizons himself maybe.

Since this was our second new guy in two years, the stakes were high. But we were certain Darren would fit right in: he loved poker, good liquor (we converted him to cheap rum), adventures of any sort, and he could tell lies. He wouldn't smoke a cigar, but all of us have one flaw. In the end, he signed on.

Oz and I arrived in Guadeloupe ahead of the others. One would think any four guys with six months' lead time could manage to arrive together. Practically never happened.

The two of us rented a car and drove all over the island waiting for Beau and Darren to show up. It turned out we're better drivers than sailors. All one needs for Caribbean driving is second gear and a horn.

Not that the noise apparently did any good: all the other cars looked like survivors from a demolition derby. We drove slowly on pavement barely linking the potholes together, got yelled at and honked at. Not to mention being the recipients of several gestures. What started out in our car sounding like a prayer meeting ended with genuine fluency in obscene responses.

An even greater challenge was right around the corner: surviving the boat orientation.

Guadeloupe is a butterfly-shaped island in the middle of the Caribbean chain with charming little islet groups off to the side and bottom of its left wing. The driving notwithstanding, it has much in common with a butterfly: colorful, graceful, gentle. It's even more French than St. Barts, and the marina guys were true Frenchmen.

Jean-Louis and Gérard. Competent sailors no doubt, and certainly friendly. But stunningly, how shall I phrase this, hygienically deficient. My three sailing buddies all disappeared as soon as Gérard came aboard.

As they headed down the dock, I shouted, "Where you guys going?" Group responses: "You can handle this without us." . . . "Just over here and grab a beer." . . . "We're redundant anyway." . . . "I've never been on a boat before." That sort of stuff. The campers had left the counselor to breathe on his own.

Walking around the boat with the Frenchman, then looking at charts together in the saloon, was a major struggle in self-control. It got worse.

"You muss shek zee o-eel eev'ry day. In zee engine rrrrroom."
No edge to his voice; just to his aura.

I responded with humble confidence, "I'm sure I can find the
dipstick."

Gérard gave me a small patronizing smile. "Eet's on zee check-
list. We ave to do eet."

One cannot truly appreciate Frenchness until you've been in a
cramped engine room with a hardworking marina hand in Guadeloupe. He wants to make damn sure the stupid Yankee sailor un-
derstands every detail. It takes awhile; and the proximity gives new
meaning to the term "cultural experience." Finally he was satisfied
with my competence, if only barely, and left.

Just before the guys returned the provisions arrived. We'd had
the locals provision the boat for this trip. Big mistake. French rum,
which we seemed to have cases of, smells and tastes much like
French perfume. We haven't actually tasted French perfume, it
might actually taste *better*. Felt we had the potential to smell like a
floating bordello.

In our humble opinion, they're putting their perfume in the
wrong place. Even our very large stock of limes could not overcome
the effects. The rum would have been better splashed on the body

than swallowed; we were thinking of recommending that to the charter guys.

Nor were there enough cookies, our main food staple, even without Alan in the crew. So we spent an hour supplementing the larder with these necessities. Air freshener was a last minute addition.

Eventually we got everyone on board the Privilege 42. Darren brought, in addition to his inexperience, his cowboy boots (two pairs), which it turns out, he wears *everywhere*. Very fancy. Rattlesnake or crocodile or something. Red swirly stitching on the sides. One black pair, one cordovan, both pointy-toed. A banker in boots. Unusual even in Colorado. Never occurred to us he'd bring them sailing.

He also brought a couple of those cream-colored cowboy shirts with brown piping along the seams, and fancy designs on the collarbone area and the back of the shoulders. Long sleeved, of course. No self-respecting cowboy would wear short sleeves even if he was playing basketball. Apparently his wife had no influence on his packing choices. Said he didn't receive the list I sent him. Obviously.

We fouled a mooring line in the prop before leaving the marina. I was at the helm. "We're not moving."

Darren had never been on a boat, and Oz's experiences were limited. So it was Beau who knowingly suggested, "Try putting both engines in forward." I'd had one in forward and one in reverse to make a tighter turn.

"Still no help."

"Damn," he responded.

I put both engines in neutral, gave him the helm and looked over the transom. "I think we've wrapped a line around the prop."

"Damn."

Darren looked at me quizzically. "What's that mean?"

"Means I go diving," I sighed.

Swimming in a marina, at least in Guadeloupe, is a unique experience, quite unlike swimming anywhere else. The water is the color of weak coffee, it smells faintly of sewage, and it feels like it's even parts water and oil, although marinas swear otherwise. In any event, a shower afterwards is mandatory. Unless, apparently, you work there.

By the time I retrieved my mask and fins, we had a rather large and amused audience. Took me three trips under water to free the line. When I finally emerged I looked like a mechanic after a long day. The charter guys were still rolling their eyes and shaking their heads. Maybe they were praying: it was hard to hear them since they were downwind. Fortunately.

Once out of the marina at Pointe-à-Pitre we sailed to Gosier Bay where we were enthralled by the dozens of little kids racing their Optimist dinghies—small bathtubs with one almost oval white sail. The natives clearly understood sailing, and the joys of throwing caution to the wind, at a much earlier age than any of us.

From there we were off to Iles de Saintes. Darren was sick most of the way there and we assured him, in usual guy fashion, that it would get worse.

"Is this what's it's supposed to be like? All this bouncing around?" he asked, looking pained. Pale too.

"Seas are pretty flat," I said, feeling overwhelmingly content. "This is perfect."

"Perfect for *what*?" he demanded. "I'm on vacation."

"Perfect for just being out here. You'll get used to it."

"Not a chance. When do we get there?" he inquired.

"Coupla hours."

"Oh gawd," he groaned. And it did get worse. For Darren.

For the rest of us the sail south was sublime. Beau and Oz were out on the bow seats, headsets on, singing loudly. Burning their backs. They had the appearance of oversized four-year-olds who'd just said goodbye to their parents.

First stop was the little group of land masses called Iles de Saintes. Captivating. Stone and mortar walls, wooden houses with red tin roofs, bougainvillea everywhere. Red, purple and fuchsia. (At least I think it was fuchsia: guys' colors tend to be basic.)

The place looked and smelled like a spring garden. Never saw a car. The whole area was just so "islandy." Darren's cowboy boots were, well, a tourist attraction. No question about our country of origin.

Fort Napoleon was fascinating with its two-foot-thick walls, creepy overgrown ammunition cells, and green iguanas about the size of Oz's arm. They were peaceful, almost shy. But it looked like they could take us apart if they ever had a meeting and decided to do so. It was hard to imagine brutal canon combat in a place so serene.

Of course the best part of this or any other place were the people, more gracious than one can imagine. One of the shop ladies recommended the crème brûlée at Le Génois in beautiful Terre de Haut. Divine. Beau now understood our new expectations.

We rented motor scooters which we drove like local maniacs. Second gear and a horn. Oz managed to wreck his so that it looked like it had been crushed by the hands of Hercules. But Darren's negotiating skills resulted in a $24 charge for a broken turn signal, though he may have promised to throw in his boots. A quick departure was in order.

It was north to Pigeon Island in the Cousteau Underwater National Park. Great snorkeling. Purple sea fans, orange and blue sponges, rust colored starfish, golden stag horn coral twisting in all directions just off the green and pink coral walls. The colors were so soft and the walls so incongruously rugged. An unimaginable variety of fish, all of which looked like they'd been painted with an entire palette of florescence.

Oz, Beau and I were in as soon as the anchor was set. Darren didn't want to go. Here's a fearless, scholarship-level jock from Yale who'd traveled everywhere including Siberia. Seems he doesn't like salt water.

After a couple of minutes, Beau popped up and yelled to him. "Ya gotta see this, Darren. Take off your boots."

"I don't know what's down there."

"Nothing harmful or we wouldn't be in the water. Besides, it's a park."

"Lotsa little fish?"

"Thousands."

"That's what *big* fish eat. Besides, I can't swim."

Group responses: "You gotta be kidding." . . . "A big jock like you?" . . . "Did you mention that when you said you wanted to come?"

"I thought we were going to sail, not swim."

Beau was not going to let him off. "We're not swimming. We're just floating along looking. Put on some flippers."

"I can't get my boots off."

We thought that might actually be true. So I crawled out to see if I could get Darren to crawl in. The first task was to get some lotion on him. He was in a lot better shape than George but had the same skin type. Red hair. Very pink body.

Actually it was worse. Under all that cover-everything cowboy garb he was blindingly white. Only his freckles had any color. However, it had become, albeit reluctantly, easier to slap lotion on another guy's back. As long as you did it quick and haphazardly.

Not that it mattered much: Darren insisted upon being encased in not one but two lifejackets. They covered *every*thing from the waist up. He was so buoyant he could barely get his face under water.

Once in though, Darren found he loved all that colorful, exotic fish and plant life. Said he felt like he was suspended over a huge aquarium. Actually, he sounded remarkably like Alan with his binoculars in Colombier Bay: "Incredible. Unbelievable. I'm never leaving."

It's odd how you can spend all day looking at fish you'd never harm, then be starving for a seafood dinner that night. Must be some sort of cranial disconnect. Edible fish have no charm. The dinners we had at the Dive Restaurant overlooking the park and our boat somehow made the visit to Cousteau all the more worthwhile.

But we couldn't resist Iles de Saintes, so we sailed back. Beau decided to give trolling a shot. We'd never caught our dinner before and it seemed possible: fairly slow sailing in an area where we'd been told there were plenty of fish.

We brought the dinghy up and tied it alongside. Then Beau rigged his pole with a beautiful white and blue lure. It looked too big, but he stated confidently that its size would keep the smaller fish from bothering us. The lure trailed along about a foot under water, 50 or so meters astern.

Nothing ever hit it. Well, to be precise, no *fish* ever hit it. A large brown cormorant did. Dove right down, scooped it up, then resurfaced and sought to relax on the surface. Before anyone could tell Beau, who had moved to the helm, he heard the line stripping and yelled, "Ha! Got one!"

The cormorant was a mini-version of the lobster trap. And we were equally alarmed, but for obviously different reasons. This bird was being dragged through the water at about five knots by its bill. We headed up immediately and furled the jib. Beau began slowly reeling in.

Darren held up his beer can like a microphone. "Now, ladies and gentlemen in our listening audience, we've managed to corner, direct from the North American offshore fishing championships, this year's gold medal winner. Tell us, Beau: how'd you manage to do it?" He shoved the can toward Beau.

Oz grabbed the mike. "Hold on, Darren. We found out this guy's a fraud. He cheats. At the championships he actually wrapped up his dog in newspaper and tried to have it weighed as his catch."

Darren brought the mike back. "Whoa there, Oz. Are you saying this world-respected angler actually tried to pass off another animal as a *fish*?"

Beau just kept slowly reeling in.

"Well," said Oz. "In the Deep South where Beau does most of his angling, some folks are known to eat most anything. If you put enough fat in that fryer, it all looks like fish."

"I'll be damned," said Darren. "The guy's been gettin' by all these years on his intimidating size alone."

By now the bird was at the transom. I jumped down on the swim platform and scooped it up. Cormorants are, up close and personal, *very* large. Surprisingly strong too. I felt like I was trying to embrace a live turkey. Not that I've actually embraced a turkey, but that was the sensation.

And this bird was seriously upset. Perhaps because of the large hook through its bill. Or maybe because he (she?) was half drowned being dragged through the water. In any event, "flailing" would be a *kind* word to describe his behavior. Twice he managed to escape my grip, and it finally took two of us to subdue him.

The actual extraction took less than a minute. And when we put him back in the water, he took off in an instant, never looking back.

Soothing words to Beau soon followed. "Ted Williams you're not." ... "I've heard you don't even need to go sailing to catch birds; but that's probably just a stupid rumor." ... "I've actually never seen a flying fish before." ... "Remind me to take a closer look at your meatloaf before I dig in."

Beau gave us one of his slanty-eyed stares, put away his line, and returned to the helm. Never said a word. He knew: we were gonna get a lot of mileage from this one.

We arrived at Iles de Saintes in time for some sort of carnival: mostly black men in white sheets, which seemed a nice juxtaposition. Several drums. One horn. We didn't see anyone in cowboy boots. And we carefully avoided the scooter shop.

Next day we had to head back to Pointe-à-Pitre, but there was a highlight left to come: we spent our last night ashore at the Holiday Inn which, it turns out, permits topless sun bathing. Sorry, Alan. We stayed an extra day. Besides, we had to talk about next year.

"If we ever do this again," Darren announced, examining the can of beer in his hand, "I'm staying right here."

"Bullshit," said Beau, rotating in his lounge chair to get a better view of the scenery. "You're no longer a sailing virgin. Worst is behind you."

"Doubt it," responded Darren, whose eyes had locked on to a young passer-by. "I'll just sit right here and wave as you sail past the beach."

"Look, Darren," I offered. "They're never gonna let you sit out here in your swim trunks and boots like we do. May as well be sailing."

"Happy to trade the boots for a chair that stays in one place. Especially *this* place."

He was kidding. We think.

Those post-sailing conversations on Guadeloupe carried over to our post-trip picture gathering back home, which, like the pre-trip get-togethers, we just called "trip meetings."

Always at the same restaurant, we exchanged our various photos, editing those unfit for friends and spouses. In fact, we discovered there are three categories of guys' trip pictures: those for the scrapbook, those the lab refuses to develop, and those which they'll develop but you can't show anyone. Lots of wasted film.

The meetings had become part of a growing set of rituals: crew shirts, lime transportation, visors, discussions about who to invite if a regular was absent (unanimity was essential), what Dave Barry book to bring along for evening entertainment, who was bringing the cigars and the port, when to go, where, for how long, and what boat might work.

Actually, the Dave Barry matter deserves special mention. He's our favorite writer. In our opinion, a literary Jimmy Buffett. (We'd become experts on cigars and French rum, why not literature?) On every trip we brought along one of his books. *Dave Barry's Complete Guide to Guys* was our favorite, but we loved others like *Dave Barry Turns 40* and *Dave Barry's Guide to Marriage and/or Sex* (of course).

About midnight, when we were tired of poker, cigars and port, one of us would read a couple of chapters. We laughed 'till we hurt. Or we pulled out the *If* book, if we weren't brain dead, and got philosophical. Either one created the atmosphere needed to drift out onto the foredeck and look at the stars.

Between Barry, the *If* questions and trying to identify constellations, we had plenty of catalysts for putting some of life's big questions into perspective. The stars reminded us of the wonder of the universe, how little we know, and how little we *are*. Barry delivered just the right amount of irreverence, especially with George gone. And *If* got us to reflect on questions we had mostly avoided: who we were and what we valued, what we loved or resented, what we dreamed about, what made us proud or ashamed, what we wanted out of life.

Together they provided an amazing adhesive to four disparate sailors. And they got us thinking about education in an entirely different light. Maybe Tania's options were *both* right, though not always easy. Wisdom? Sometimes you gotta row your dinghy and drag your boat.

Inevitably on each trip we came to the realization we were living our version of Tania's adventure, leaving our own little harbors behind. Doing something bigger, and along the way, *thinking* bigger. It felt really good.

What's more, we discovered that anticipation truly *is* almost as wonderful as being there. We could spend all year looking forward to the next trip, not knowing and not caring exactly where and when it would be. The next trip gave us a great excuse to get together.

Some of the meetings seemed longer than the trips. But we laughed a lot and argued little. We still sought adventure, but the whole thing had become an *event*. An annual escape from all guilt. Maybe it hadn't become the center of our lives, but it was close. No one wanted *The Carnival* to stop.

5

The Grenadines

One of the best temporary cures for pride and affectation is seasickness.

—Henry Wheeler Shaw

All of the post- and pre-trip stuff had become institutionalized by this time: meeting at least once to reminisce and share photos, then immediately planning the next meeting, unencumbered by pictures but burdened with ideas and charts. My role as camp counselor was fully developed by now: convene the meetings, bring all the stuff, try to keep everyone on task, prepare to be ignored.

Oz needed a year off for professional reasons, and Alan was back in, so it was Alan, Beau, Darren, and me (Flaky, Studly, Boots and Scout) who met to decide that year's destination.

The discussion was particularly lively.

"I don't care where we go," said Alan. "Or when. So long as we go." His motive remained *escape*.

"I don't care either," contributed Beau, "as long as it's five days. That's my 'fun' quotient."

"As long as it's new," Darren added. "I never go anywhere twice. Waveless would be a nice feature too. No motion whatsoever even better."

"So long as you three guys are there, I don't care either," I said sweetly. Which prompted Alan to pour the last ounce of his beer on my lap. I fleetingly thought of reciprocating, but he was wearing an ancient pair of checked flannel slacks, and I wasn't sure he'd notice. Especially with the paint stains already there.

In truth I still had exploration as an essential element, and I was ready with articles, charts and persuasion. It didn't take much, once we worked out the timing.

We chose to head for the Grenadines in the Windward Islands. New challenges and quieter anchorages were high on the priority list that year. Naïveté and courage were overflowing. I almost felt like phoning Tania.

It didn't take long to resolve the usual issues of who'd be responsible for bringing the Barry books, limes, cigars and port. Surprisingly, the Guadeloupe experience had not dulled our courage in letting the charter company provision the boat with food and liquor. Grenada isn't French; all we needed to do was spell out some preferences. Beau made most of them.

We flew into Grenada to pick up the Lagoon 3700 catamaran. The trip began with bad omens. Engine problems kept us in Mount Hartman Bay an extra half day, so we didn't get far on Day One.

True Blue Bay is just an hour or so from the marina. Needing sustenance, we thought we'd grill some steaks for our first night. The first task was attaching the grill to the stern rail. Darren and I took on the chore; Alan kept our cups full.

It was a solid, rectangular grill, not one of those light round aluminum things on most charter boats. Darren held it in place with both hands and a knee. I fumbled with the attachments.

In a matter of seconds, we inadvertently dropped it overboard. *Big* splash. Fifteen feet of water. Immediately out of sight. It had been dark for over an hour.

By now expecting flawless crew performance, I asked pointedly, "Didn't you have a grip on it?"

Darren, sounding rather bankeresque, said, "I thought you did."

"I was putting on the wing nuts. How could I be gripping?"

"Well, I was counting on gripping, not griping."

"Damn," said Alan, resident life observer, who was peering overboard. "Sunk faster'n a stone. Wish I'd had my camera."

Then came Beau's voice from the galley below: "When will the coals be ready?"

So we ate ashore. Indigo's saved our evening. Deliciously, I might add. It was a quintessentially Caribbean restaurant. Poled up on this hill overlooking True Blue Bay, which itself looked like a postcard. Indigo's was white with blue trim, and a matching blue roof. Spotless. Eating was mainly on the balcony with its white and blue railing, hanging out over the hillside. Mostly fish on the menu, which was mostly what we wanted anyway. Exquisite preparation. Take note, Beau.

The bonus was we were close enough that our charter company was able to deliver us a new grill by jeep early the next morning. They were upbeat about the whole thing: "It happens all the time." If they only knew.

We weighed anchor and left about 8:00 but failed to secure the anchor sufficiently. About an hour after departure it, along with ten meters of chain and a whole lot of rode, bounced off the bow roller and plunged overboard. Retrieved with much sweat but without incident, however. Nice that it didn't catch the bottom since we were under sail. Not *much* sail, thankfully.

Sailing up Grenada's west coast to Carriacou was arduous. Wind right on the nose (where the hell were the prevailing easterlies?), seas maybe 5-6 feet, and in that cat we had to work hard to make any progress at all.

Half of us got sick. It was the half with prior experience, however, so it came easily. Almost enthusiastically, it seemed to Beau and me. Then the dinghy, which we were towing, swamped.

Fortunately, we'd had the good sense to detach the dinghy's motor when we left True Blue Bay and attach it firmly (hey, we didn't want another grill experience) to our stern rail. So it was only the top of the inflatable which was level with the water. We stopped, shortened the tow line, which was one helluva lot of work, and convened a meeting.

It was only Darren's second trip, and he was very sick. The yacht was bobbing like a cork. He looked awful. And helpless. "Now what? I can't stand this very long."

I couldn't either. "We gotta get that water out of there. Can't drag a sea anchor all the way to Carriacou. Slow enough already. We're lucky the line's still attached."

Beau was still feeling way too energetic. "Maybe I can stand on the swim platform and turn it over."

I was incredulous. "Do you have any idea how heavy that thing is filled with water?"

"Just hold my belt."

"You're nuts. It's not a lobster trap."

"Did I miss something?" groaned Darren.

"Yeah. The first trip."

In the end, we dragged it along the starboard side of the cat and hooked a spinnaker halyard to its nose. Then winched it to vertical to empty it. This all took about twenty minutes during which, as fate would have it, two boats passed us going south who found the sight rather amusing. We could see them pointing and laughing: ninnies in action. People even came on deck from down below, cameras in hand.

Alan was so weak he could barely stand, but he too found the episode hysterical. He was lurching around laughing, throwing up, trying to steady his camera with both hands without falling over-board. Must have shot half a roll of film. And lost about five pounds.

Soon we were underway again, however; and just as soon, the other two of us got sick. As the saying goes, you've either been sea-sick or you will be. It was now unanimous.

We almost applauded when the black rock of Carriacou began to emerge. Tyrrel Bay, where we stopped for the night, was never more welcome. The dinghy was floating. We reattached the motor; it ran perfectly. All four of us were mobile. Food was even beginning to sound good again. Didn't take long for veterans like us.

It wasn't a day to end with a Barry book, though. Nothing seemed too funny. Even poker was short-lived. We collapsed in our bunks. The gentle lapping of the water against the hulls was heard for, maybe, two minutes. Getting sick is exhausting.

Revived the next day, we popped into Union Island, cleared customs, and left. Never got comfortable there. For completely mysterious reasons, we felt we had to lock the boat, lock the dinghy when we went ashore, keep our hands on our money.

Irrational, probably, since Union Island has a charter base, and tourists are plentiful. But the *feeling* was a world apart from Iles de Saintes. Detached and indifferent. Besides, we had no reason to stay and we wanted to do some sailing on flat water.

Our first stop was to see John Caldwell on Palm Island since we were all fans of *Desperate Voyage*, his book about single-handedly crossing the Pacific to Australia. It was just after World War II, and he was determined to reunite with a girl he'd met when he was serving in the navy. Very romantic. Full of courage, adventure. Our kind of reading.

We stopped in the gift shop, festooned with shirts, hats, visors, shorts, dresses and swim suits, in the brightest colors imaginable. Stripes, solids, polka dots; you name it. Many were hanging on strings draped from one beam to another, just below the ceiling. Shells, carvings, paintings, koozies and film jammed the shelves. The whole shop had this marvelous smell. Gardenias, I think.

A very friendly lady, dressed in an explosion of red and yellow print, was behind the counter. Pink hibiscus bloom tucked just over her right ear. Incredibly white teeth. Beau asked her if John was on the island.

"Yessuh, sho is," she said with a big smile, and rang him up. We were feeling lucky.

Five minutes later he arrived. A wiry guy somewhere past 70, probably short of 80. Hard to tell. Dark thinning hair. Skin the color of a cup of good English tea, which at the time he was holding in a beat-up white mug. (Okay, we're not sure it was tea.) He looked worn out, but he certainly didn't sound that way, and he offered to show us around his island.

"Do I know you guys?" he asked, kind of cocking his head to one side.

"No," I said. "We've read your book and wanted to meet you."

"Been a long time," he smiled. "Glad you remembered. I'm flattered."

We had our books with us, and Beau asked, "Mind autographing a few copies?"

"Hell no. Honored," John responded, and smiled again.

Darren didn't have one, and only knew about John through our descriptions about who he was and what he'd done. Probably a good thing: you tend to see the ocean through different eyes after reading it. Hurricanes. Sharks. Destruction on an atoll. We'd edited our remarks for Darren.

When John was done signing, we rather shyly asked him a few more questions. "Did you really land a shark that crushed your transom?"

"I did kill a shark once."

"How about drinking motor oil and eating belt leather to stay alive?"

He just grinned.

"Okay," I asked, "how about cormorant?"

Beau elbowed me so hard I almost fell over. John just looked at me quizzically. Then he remembered he needed to meet with his plumber or something, so he shook hands all around and left. We toured the small island on our own, talking to whomever we met as we walked.

Turns out the voyage wasn't quite as desperate as "Coconut Johnny" had written. But he was still fascinating and the island was beautiful. It's become a very fashionable tropical retreat: several small cream-colored cottages sprinkled through the lush vegetation, each with its own private stretch of beach. The infrastructure stuff, like water tanks and generators, are in the center and hidden by plantings. Lovely and serene.

Matter of fact, the entire Caribbean chain is more beautiful because of John's planting all those palm trees on the islands when he was hauling freight between them. Assuming, of course, there's truth in *that* story. One never knows when it comes to ol' John. But now that he's gone, we're glad we made the trip to share some lies and have him sign our books.

Somewhere along our walk Alan asked, "Did I miss something? I don't recall John ever eating a bird on his trip."

"Nah," I said. "That was a left-handed reference to last year. What you don't realize is that Beau here does an exquisite job with fresh cormorant."

"Downright sinful," nodded Darren.

"Actually," said Beau, "that's all crap. It just happened that a bird tried to commit suicide while I was fishing."

"Sorry I missed it," said Alan. He was even sorrier after Darren and I relayed the whole story, embellishing as necessary. We all nearly doubled up with laughter. Even Beau.

After Palm Island we ducked up to Canouan for a night, then back to Mayreau and Salt Whistle Bay, right on the northern tip of the island. Beautiful half-moon cove. Sand so white with pink flecks it reminded one of, well, George or Darren when the sun was just right. Hurt your eyes to look at it. Ringed by palms. Between the palm trees over a small spit of land, Canouan is beautiful about four miles north.

The bay was completely empty of other boats when we were there. It has to be one of the most idyllic places in the world. Except when it rains, which it did for two days and three nights. Depressing effect on cigar smoking.

We played a lot of poker, though we were no longer using matchsticks for money. Alan brought along real chips this time. We bought them for nickels, dimes and quarters. Mostly played goofy dealer's choice games; a huge pot was maybe $5.

"Okay," I said. "Low hole, high spade."

"What's that?" Alan asked.

"The same game it was in Colombier. Not that you were paying attention. Lusting after flesh has a distracting effect."

"No need for moralizing, Tom. Just remind me of the rules."

We played that and Night Baseball, Texas Hold 'Em, Draw. Even a game or two of Indian. Darren won a bit more than equity might suggest, mostly at my expense. But even when it was all over, the exchange didn't amount to a case of beer. We had fun, as ever. Still, after two whole days we got real tired of it.

We read some. And early one evening we talked about John Caldwell, sitting out on the trampoline between rain squalls with a fine port and some very large cigars.

Beau was really impressed. "That guy did amazing things. No resources, no skills—at least at the beginning. He taught himself to sail, bought an old tub, and proceeded to take off across the Pacific Ocean. Just to fulfill a commitment to a girl."

"I think he was crazy," said Darren, who wasn't smoking but may as well have been, the air was so thick. He just couldn't seem to get upwind, and every time he moved he spilled more of his drink.

"I think he was in love," I countered. "Love makes you crazy." Very philosophical exhale.

"He only got crazy after he was out there," Beau added thoughtfully. "And that's a different kind of crazy. Love and courage got him to do it."

"Sure was resourceful," I added. "No matter what the Pacific threw at him, he coped. Like Tania said, 'Just get up and keep going. Otherwise you aren't going to get home.' Life ain't gonna be all downhill."

Alan nodded while tipping a bit more port into everyone's glasses. "In a way, the guy's a *lot* like Tania. Got a dream? Throw off the lines and just go for it. What have you got to lose?"

"Fair enough," I said. "That's what we're doing in our own way. We lose a lot more if we just sit on our butts. Those two are different, though. Seems to me it's a *huevos* issue: just how much balls do you have? Tania didn't even have the love part. Pure guts."

"More like curiosity, maybe," offered Alan, who had now settled back against the mast. "Guts is opting for college and landing in one of your classes."

I smiled. "That's where the naïveté comes in."

"There may be another way to look at this," Alan reflected. "Tania and John were both naïve in their own way. They went sailing alone and gained wisdom. Adventure just got in their way."

I picked up the line. "So here we are, older and wiser, seeking adventure by acting young and stupid. Those two played it forward. Our dream is just being twenty again for a week, guilt free."

"Not exactly my point," said Alan. "The dreams are the same except in magnitude. It's the perspective that's different. We know what we're getting into."

Beau had been quiet for several minutes, thoroughly enjoying his cigar since he had picked it out. "Are courage and stupidity proportionate?" he asked.

"If Alan's right, only for the young," I responded.

Darren changed from one bow seat to the other, still trying to stay upwind. For quite awhile he seemed detached from the conversation, looking like he was contemplating a rise in mortgage rates. He surprised us with his re-entry. "Like banking. There's room for some courage, but none for stupidity or naïveté. Adult world. It's all about risk assessment."

"Damn," said Alan. "That makes us pretty wimpy. No risk in sight here."

It was silent for quite awhile. "I dunno," I finally said. "We have our dreams. We're pursuing them. We may not be Tania or John, but we made a commitment even if it wasn't particularly courageous. May have been naïve though. Takes a certain amount of courage just to get on a boat with you three."

"Not to mention," said Alan, "the courage to eat Beau's cooking."

We all laughed and decided it was time for dinner. Ashore. But John Caldwell re-opened some of the questions we first confronted with Tania. And in one form or another, surfaced every year.

The Salt Whistle Bay Club is the only establishment anywhere near this anchorage, and so well hidden in the vegetation it's easily missed. But we'd studied our cruising guide as always, and dinghied in for dinner. The German manager there, Undine, is, at first impression, *really* German. Tall, blond, straight-backed, a bit austere. But she took one look at Darren's boots and cracked up.

"Do you always wear those sailing?" she asked. "Or only in wet weather?" Any German accent had been nearly obliterated by living in the Caribbean.

"Heard it might flood," Darren responded. If he was offended it didn't show. "Wanted to be prepared. Wore boots. Even brought a spare pair."

"Real practical on board, I'd guess," she said with a nice bit of sarcasm. "They match your shorts?"

"Proper cowpoke never wears shorts, ma'am," Darren responded. "But if I did, I reckon I could park m'boots awhile." This Coloradoan was now sounding Texan. Fake Texan.

"Don't let him jerk your chain, Undine," said Beau. "He wears those things to bed. We think."

After that, we all became friends. The food and service were great, but then, there were no other diners. We decided all other charterers were a bunch of fair weather sailors. Wimps.

During one small break in the clouds we managed to walk over to Saline Bay with the mandatory stop at Dennis's Hideaway for a beverage. Must have been arduous in those boots, but Darren never mentioned it.

The real drag was that the rain kept us from ever getting to the Tobago Cays for the superb snorkeling. Bummer, since that was the biggest attraction for choosing the Grenadines to begin with. We vowed to return (but never did).

We had to return to Union Island where my three companions were getting off to go home. Not our favorite place. Indifference had given way to passion. There was some sort of civil protest in full force when we arrived, and we had the very distinct look of outsiders: pale bodies, matching shirts. We ducked into a bar to escape.

Great steel drum music inside, and we love pan music. It was well into the evening hours on a weekend, and the crowd looked as though it had been drinking for days. There was even a limbo contest going on, but with only one contestant. Native guy who kept going under the bar with a beer can balanced on his forehead.

"Damn," said Alan. "That guy's really good."

"Good and drunk," offered Beau, who'd seen enough and turned his back.

"I don't think so," Alan responded. "If he was drunk, he'd fall over."

Beau never turned around. "Okay then. He's a professional."

"You're full of it," said Alan. "Even on *this* island you can't make a living as a limbo dancer," apparently thinking Beau might have been serious. Still, Alan looked like he was getting ready to take a picture of the guy.

Beau saw him out of the corner of his eye and grabbed his arm, so the flash wouldn't draw attention. "Anything's possible. Remember *Don't Stop the Carnival.*"

The guy *was* good, even if only slightly more sober than the onlookers.

In the hour we were there the intensity level noticeably increased. The music got louder, smells became more pungent, customers got rowdier. The atmosphere got scarier. Celebration was beginning to border on conflict. We decided to pass on the great music in the interests of self-preservation.

Next day the guys left and I was joined by my wife and two other couples. The plan was another week of sailing, then return the yacht to Grenada. First time I'd done that, though it became a tradition of its own. The catamaran was the draw: Linda does not like her boats well heeled, as a punster might put it, so the cat provided a perfect opportunity for her to join me.

The timing was perfect. All the poker, lies and gas, and most of the craziness, was out of my system. The cigars were gone. Worked out great. Lungs needed a break by then anyway.

This bonus never seemed to have an adverse impact on the guys. They were envious of my extra week on the water; but they all wanted their reunions to be on land. Particularly Darren.

In the end it wasn't our favorite guys' trip. The thrill of meeting Coconut Johnny just couldn't offset getting sick, getting rain, feeling creepy on Union Island, and *not* getting to snorkel the Tobago Cays. Even before we got back, Darren said "Never again. All these islands look alike, especially in the rain."

This time he was dead serious. We'd miss the boots. But it wasn't gonna stop the rest of us.

6

The British Virgins

Flatter not yourself that good luck is judgment and discretion, for all your eggs could have foundered if the spirit of the sea had just said the word.

—Herman Melville

Darren came to the post-trip meeting of course, so we exchanged pictures and jokes. He remained firm in his resolve not to go again. Maybe he was tired of being sick on his vacations.

Only a couple of months later we were working on #6. Darren had departed but Oz was back. He, Beau, Alan and I were in familiar territory in the planning meetings, but the discussions were a bit different this time.

Right out of the box Beau suggested, "Let's go the British Virgin Islands."

I was shocked. "Why? I lived there. You've been there. Everybody sails there. Where's the adventure in that?" Two things bothered me immediately. One was that my need to *discover* on these trips, to challenge ourselves with the unknown, was at risk. The second was a fear that we'd lost sight of Tania's message altogether. We would go on a vacation, not an exploration.

Beau is a tough customer when he has made up his mind. Especially, like all of us perhaps, when it is his idea. "People go there because it's a great place to go. Besides, Alan and Oz haven't seen 'em. Everyone ought to sail the BVIs at least once."

Shock turned to dismay. "I've probably sailed those islands a dozen times." That just seemed to raise the other two's curiosity.

Oz had a quizzical look on his face. "Why would you sail them that much if they weren't great?"

"Well," I said, trying not to sound blasé but probably failing, "they are great, and the sailing's terrific. They're just crowded. They're, well, pedestrian. People go there who don't know how to raise a sail. No-brainer sailing."

Oz sat back just a bit. With only two trips under his belt plus a two-year layoff, he clearly liked that idea and it showed in his expression. "Nothing the matter with that."

Alan had been following this brief exchange intently, leaning into it as he frequently did. "Nude beaches?"

"Nope," I said casually. "They're English, Alan. If anything, the BVIs are the most conservative place we've ever gone." I watched the disappointment form on his face.

Alan sat straight up and announced, "Okay, I'm with Tom. Let's do Martinique."

But in the end, we did decide on the BVIs. Maybe the adventurous spirit had waned. Maybe we just got lazy. Before the meeting was over I had a sneaking feeling it was the beginning of the end. The others were happy as clowns.

The BVIs *do* have advantages, though nudity's not one of them: great restaurants, beautiful islands, and easy anchorages, nearly all of which are protected from the easterly winds and exposed to astonishing sunsets in the evenings. Only short reaches between them too, where even nuts like us wouldn't be far from rescue. Not that we ever needed one. Boat choices were limitless. One could be comfortable *and* guilt-free.

Alan was always quick to find ways of injecting new life into the adventures, especially if he thought the commitment of one of us was less than his. Which was total. Our list of "traditions" seemed to increase every time we went, often as not because of some new idea Alan had.

This year he added yet another one: customized CDs. Alan painstakingly collected, over a period of months, what each of us identified as our favorite sailing songs (heavily tilted toward practically everything Jimmy Buffett ever recorded), then made an individual CD for each of us.

It wasn't *all* Buffett. I, of course, tended toward John Denver, whereas Oz wanted Mick Jagger. (I'll never understand Mick Jagger or theoretical math, much less how one person can love both.) Collectively we had tastes running from Bach to the Beach Boys, with practically everything in between. Alan worked it all out.

We gave all four of those CDs a lot of airtime. It didn't matter that Jimmy Buffett had 10-12 songs on every one of them. We never tired of his singing about what we were doing.

There was an unexpected bonus to these CDs: they bring back a flood of great memories when played at home. Cheap way to visit the islands.

We all left Colorado on the same plane, did the usual transfers in San Juan, and arrived together in the BVIs. Remarkable: it only happened once.

The first night on Tortola was spent in a hotel. Well, two of us did. Oz sleep walks (fortunately not when we're sailing). I found him wandering around the hotel grounds in the middle of the night. Happily, he had not fallen into the pool. Tried to wake him, but to no avail. That did not keep him from talking, however. Seemed creepy: walking and talking without waking up.

"Oz, do you know where you are?" I asked, sort of holding onto him by the upper arm.

"Juss takin' a walk. Relaxin'. No problem." He was lurching around, but it didn't seem like he was going to fall over.

I tried looking him right in the eyes, which were open but blank. "Do you know what country you're in?"

"Juss takin' a walk. No problem," he said, lunging forward a bit.

The question seemed to have no influence on the answer. Somehow I coaxed him back into the room. He went right back to bed. Never got up again. Never stopped talking either. I was awake and silent; he was asleep and talking. Odd.

Not ten minutes later Beau knocked on our door and said he'd lost Alan. Seems he simply drifted off after dinner and didn't return. Lots of activity in Road Town on a Friday night. Where would he go? *Why?* Out looking for artistic inspiration?

Beau and I had a rather sleepy discussion about what to do (Oz seemed content in bed and we weren't going to mess with that), but ultimately decided looking for Alan was futile. He showed up before the sun. Good thing: we didn't want to wait for him *again*.

In a certain sense, we'd gotten used to Alan's wandering tendencies. On previous trips he would, unannounced, just swim or dinghy ashore and disappear for hours. Almost like he wasn't satisfied regressing to twenty; he wanted to just keep going all the way to two.

We never knew where he went or when he'd be back. It made Beau furious. But after a while we shrugged and chalked it up to an artist's need to have a deeply personal experience. Still, we wished we'd had him drag a long string.

Anyway, after breakfast Beau and I went to a local supermarket to do the provisioning. Now one not familiar with the Caribbean might not know that power outages are regular occurrences. At least weekly when I lived there. No lights, no TV, no fans, no washer/dryer. No ironing either, not that I noticed.

On this occasion we had nearly filled two shopping carts when it suddenly all went dark. Very dark. You-have-been-buried-alive dark.

"Beau, where are you?" It wasn't a shout exactly, but I did raise my voice.

"Not sure. Somewhere behind you, I think. Near the cookies."

"Figures. But I don't remember where they were."

"Couple of isles back. I'll keep talking 'till you find me."

"No doubt. Try not to eat all the cookies before we get out of here."

"Can't promise that. But I won't have 'em all eaten before you find me. Plus I think this shelf's full of 'em."

Only in the front of the store could you see if you still had your own cart. With sight gone, tactile and oral communication rose. It began with groping and several expletives, then escalated to loud talking, stumbling, even a few shouts.

The registers were dead, having been electric when they were alive. Not even a working hand calculator in this store. Checkout was done manually, meaning the clerk added up items on a pad with a pencil. Evidence suggested this clerk excelled, when in school, in English or geography.

Everyone in line, the very *long* line, pitched in so that we all managed exact change. By touch or words we learned more about our fellow shoppers than we ever really wanted to know. What began as a brief, necessary trip became a three-hour cultural experience in togetherness.

Fact is, grocery shopping in the islands is never quite like home. Two unique features stand out. First, items are stocked randomly. You're just as likely to find the coffee with personal hygiene products as you are to find it with beverages. Forget about that highly organized shopping list: you're gonna get a week's worth of exercise making five or six loops through that store looking for *something*. Makes you wish you were *in* the cart.

Second, ever wonder what happens to all that ugly fruit and brown lettuce they can't sell at home? It's taken on a second life in the islands. At twice the price. Kinda tilts you toward canned goods. They're *three* times the price, but at least you're not whining about appearance. Just your bill.

Undaunted, we loaded up our very precious provisions and took a cab to the marina.

For the second straight year we were on a Lagoon 3700 cat, with one short straw in the saloon: there were only three real beds. We opted to begin with a clockwise circle of Tortola out of Road Town, so we spent the first night at Cane Garden Bay.

The cruising guides accurately describe Cane Garden as one of the most beautiful anchorages in the BVIs. Shaped like a backwards-facing "C," it provides excellent protection from the easterlies. A white palm-fringed beach stretches its entire length. At one end there's a palm tree that had grown up a couple of feet, then out to the side several more before heading skyward again. Bet hundreds of honeymooners had perched on that tree and sent the photo home to envious families. One place for us *not* to waste a shot.

Fifty meters away, Rhymer's Bar and Grill sits right on the beach, along with a string of other dining and drinking options. All of them open air. The buildings never look quite permanent.

Pour a slab of concrete. Build a square bar on it. Put a shaky-looking superstructure over the top. Cover the sides with large wooden panels that look like garage doors, hinged so you can lift them when there's no hurricane. Staple up some old T-shirts left by former drunks. Bingo. Caribbean night life.

But only a few of the places in Cane Garden have live music; Rhymer's is one of them. That night it was really jumping: pan music from the band, rock on the stereo during their breaks. The dance floor was jammed.

"Remind you of any place?" I had to sort of lean over the table and yell.

"All they need's a limbo guy," Alan shouted back.

"Lots better here," Beau suggested with a smile. "I'm feeling so damn good I might even get up and dance."

"Don't," said Oz, gesturing with his beer. "There's no doctor in the house."

"Even if you survived," I said, with as much haughtiness as I could muster, "you'd embarrass the hell out of all of us."

It was really loud though, and conversation was difficult, save for some quick one-liners. Eventually we even gave that up.

So after dinner we indulged in people watching, exchanged knowing grins regarding certain dancers, smoked our usual cigars. When, even with the sea breeze, the smells of sweat and beer and ashtrays overcame the salt air, we left. Not early, but it was still dark. The dinghy's autopilot got us back to the cat. No one remembers with precision.

Next day we were off to Marina Cay, then onto The Dogs for some snorkeling. Went there because we'd heard a private plane had once gone down on the south side of Great Dog. The story was it had become, with time, a fascinating artificial reef. We spent two futile hours looking. No coral, few fish, no plane. Maybe some diving pilot jumped in and flew away.

A day later we headed up to Gorda Sound, using the western entrance, which is a bit like a canyon-rafting experience in Colorado. There's skinny water off Anguilla Point where it's most narrow; no problem for a catamaran. Still, I like to err on the side of caution.

"Hey, Beau." I had to shout since his CD headset was turned up so loud I'd been singing along to "A Pirate Looks at Forty." All of us know every word. Secretly we think Buffett wrote it for *us*. "Can you come over and give me continuous readings off the depth sounder? I want to concentrate on my bearing." He moved over from the other side of the cockpit, punched off his CD.

"No problem. 6, 6, 6, 6, 6 . . ."

"That can't be right. I know this channel better than that. It changes."

He kept staring at the instruments. "I'm reading what's there: 6, 6, 6, 6 . . ."

A light bulb went on. "Check again. What are you reading?"

"Oops, sorry. It was our speed." I'd never before seen Beau looking sheepish. Even now he looked more indifferent than apologetic.

"Great. That'll tell us how far onto the reef we'll go when we hit."

However, we made it.

It was December and the Denver Broncos were in the NFL playoffs so we headed for the Bitter End Yacht Club where we were sure they'd be on TV. No luck; but it turned out we could get the game on the boat's radio, about five seconds of every twenty. Four guys huddled around the radio, playing poker with less than adequate concentration. Random questions broke the silence, along with much static.

"Did he say third down?"

"Who was the holding call on?"

"Are we winning or losing?"

"At poker, or on the field?"

"Doesn't really matter. It's out of our hands, though my hand stinks."

"They'd rather be *here* anyway. Freezing there."

"Dead right. I'll go for two."

"Two points or two cards?"

"Pass the port."

Some days one feels a bit like Pigpen in the Peanuts cartoons: there's this dark cloud that won't seem to go away. On this trip the transmission cable broke just below the shift lever.

That made for an easy decision on where to go that day: nowhere, unless you're comfortable only with sails. We're not, especially with someone else's boat, so we made up a batch of Bloody Marys. The charter company was very responsive and we lost less than a day. The mechanic thought the Marys were great.

Beau was sure we could fish on the reef north of Mosquito Island, a half mile or so away. We grabbed a mooring in Leverick Bay, dropped off Alan and Oz ashore for a hike (counting on Oz to hold the string), and dinghied over. Downwind. Easy trip.

We'd been puttering along for quite awhile, looking for a likely spot, not that I'd have recognized one. "It's further over here than I thought," I said casually, easing back on the throttle.

Beau, ever the confident angler, responded, "Yeah, but we're gonna catch dinner." He was in the front of the dinghy, keeping a sharp eye.

"We never have."

Beau kept his attention straight forward. "This will be different."

"I hate to be a cynic. Bet a beer? And birds don't count."

"You're on. But I already own my share of the beer."

"Okay, loser serves 'em."

"Now there's a gutsy bet," finally turning to look at me. "No wonder you lost at poker."

The dinghy motor died just before we got there and never restarted. We caught no fish, though that provided me little satisfaction. The real downer was rowing back to the yacht entirely against the wind.

"Bring back some fond memories, Beau?" I asked between pulls.

"Ah, unforgettable Simpson Bay Lagoon. Four years seems like an eternity. At least I'm dressed properly." He was working a lot less hard than I was. Size matters.

"Yeah, and there's only two of us. But last time we had a motor and some beer cans."

"I think," Beau reflected while pulling gently on his oar, "the only thing we can cheer about is that the cigars are safe aboard the yacht."

"That, and the fact that you're not whining. Sure glad this wasn't my idea."

About halfway back we happened to notice something floating on the water. It was a fish. A large slender fish, bluish silver, maybe 3 feet long. It was alive, but barely.

"What d'ya think?" I asked Beau.

"Beats what we caught."

"Or ever dreamed of catching," I noted, "since it is not flying. Let's take it back to the boat. Tell 'em we caught it."

"Great idea," said Beau. Then he grinned.

"Don't even think about it," I said. "You're still serving."

I hauled it into the dinghy where it flopped around a bit. It had rather large teeth, and kept slowly opening and closing its mouth.

"What do you suppose it is," I asked. "Kingfish?"

"Barracuda," Beau said casually.

Considering the almost languid pace of our earlier fishing efforts, my feet left the bottom of the dinghy at astonishing speed. Damn near fell overboard. Nothing like an unhappy barracuda squirming on your bare feet to focus your attention. It may have been on life support, but Grandpa B wasn't done yet. And it made the dinghy all slimy.

As we approached the yacht, I shouted to Oz, who was watching us return. "Dinner! Get a camera," and held up the fish by its gills.

When we reached the transom Oz was back, camera in hand. "Stand up and hold it," he asked excitedly, gesturing with his free hand. "Angle'd be better."

So I did. Then, in one fluid but completely uncoordinated motion, I lost my footing on all that slime and fell backwards into the water. My arms flew up and the fish went airborne, returning home.

"Graceful," remarked Beau righteously.

"9.6," yelled Oz with a grin.

The fish still laid around on the surface, but we decided not to re-land it. I was not about to press my luck with those teeth, and Oz and Beau were laughing so hard they'd have been absolutely no help. Barracudas are way too bony to eat anyway. I've heard they feel the same about us. We ate ashore.

Next day we met another boatful of Colorado guys at the Cooper Island Beach Club, which provided us with some reinforcement that we weren't totally crazy. At least not *uniquely* crazy. They'd noticed a small Colorado flag we fly off a shroud when sailing. Always a great conversation starter, as it was that day.

"Noticed your Colorado flag," one of them remarked. "We're from there too. Where do you guys live?"

Not the time for a "Cheesburger" routine. Oz and Alan said, "Lafayette." Beau added "Lyons. In the foothills north of Boulder."

"Summit County," I said coolly, guessing he'd never heard of it. "About 80 miles west of Denver."

"Know it well," said one of them. "My best friend lives there."

"You're kidding. Where does he live?"

It turned out this guy had actually been in my house before I bought it from his best friend. It's a very small world. Or maybe it's just that goofy guys hang out in the same places.

One of the other guys from that crew owned a casino in Central City, which was of great interest to Beau and Oz. But we didn't invite them over for poker.

They did come by for a drink, however. We exchanged the usual guy talk, mostly harmless lies about sailing adventures, some about Colorado. The Broncos filled our obligatory sports conversation. We didn't know them well enough, or drink enough, to get into that other area of expertise.

When they got in their dinghy to return to their boat, Oz dutifully cast them off. Unfortunately they'd not yet started their motor. The 15-knot breeze blew them about a hundred meters in the wrong direction, but by then we'd gotten in our dinghy for a retrieval mission. Hooked up and dragged 'em home. They never did get their motor going; but they were quick to point out we'd cast them off a bit hastily.

Year six wound to a close with our anchorage in The Bight at Norman Island. It's an immense bay, not too wide but very deep, and very popular, being only an hour's sail from Tortola where the charters begin and end.

We first went over to snorkel the caves where, according to legend, Robert Louis Stevenson visited before writing *Treasure Island*. At least some of the stories are true. "A letter of 1750 stated, 'Recovery of the treasure from *Nuestra Señora* buried at Norman Island, comprising $450,000 dollars, plate, cochineal, indigo, tobacco, much dug up by Tortolians.' "

Oz wasn't sure he wanted to get out of the dinghy, which we had tied to a mooring outside. "It looks too dark." He was by now a seasoned snorkeler, but this time he was clearly apprehensive.

"It *is* dark," I responded dismissively. "But once inside your eyes will adjust. It's worth it. Some say they buried thousands of cookies."

"It's not what I can see that's troublesome," said Oz. "It's what I can't see."

"Very philosophical," noted Beau, cocking a finger toward Oz. "Let's discuss that later." Then he shoved Oz into the water with a laugh.

The three caves are spectacular. Once you've snorkeled in and acclimated, they open up into large caverns. A few side channels.

Lots of little nooks and alcoves. Plenty of room to bury treasure if one was so inclined. We had none, either going in or coming out.

The Bight's a wonderful anchorage. Maybe three dozen boats in there, but they're all on separate moorings and pretty spread out. We picked up one off to one side to minimize our sense of neighborhood.

Alan had noticed the WILLIAM THORNTON, a large black schooner anchored off the south shore. By late afternoon it was already humming. "What's that?" he asked.

"The WILLIE-T," I responded. "Floating restaurant and bar. A Bight institution. Been there 30 years, I think. Nothing special, though. Trust me."

"Gets really nuts later," chipped in Beau in his usual knowledgeable tone. "Noisy. People get drunk and jump off the yardarms. Stuff like that."

"I've seen 'em doing it nude," I added, and immediately regretted it.

"Let's go," said Alan excitedly. It took us a long time to talk him out of it. No one else was interested; and we didn't want our dinghy missing all night.

Shortly thereafter, we were, at last, sitting around the cockpit having our usual rum and tonics. After a few minutes, Beau broke into a sly smile and looked my way. I knew what was coming.

"So, Tom," he said, raising his eyebrows a bit. "Just how bad was this trip?"

"Lousy. No exploration, unless you count all that grocery store groping," I responded firmly. "The only real challenge was getting into Gorda Sound with you reading the depth. It all sucked."

"You lie like road kill," Alan chimed in. "This was a great trip, even without nude women." He lit a cigar that looked like a summer sausage. Way too big for his body size.

"I agree," added Oz with a sigh. "I loved this trip. For openers, we actually began and ended together. That's a first. Stuff in between wasn't bad either." Oz's smoke of choice was considerably more modest.

"Okay, I admit it, though it's painful conceding anything to you guys," I said. "Even without new discoveries. The CDs alone were worth the trip. And there's a lot to be said for relaxing."

"Damn right," said Beau, a definite smugness in his voice. Then he turned preachy. "Vacation and relaxation are not mutually exclusive undertakings. You got rid of the rest of the guilt. Get rid of that part too."

"Being young and stupid feels right good," suggested Oz, exhaling gently. "May actually be a periodic necessity."

"That settles it," Alan stated with finality. "We're never going home."

Amidst lively discussion about how desirable, and ridiculous, that idea was, we were interrupted by the arrival of a barge-like powerboat named DELIVERANCE. DELIVERANCE is in helpful service as a mobile provisioner: a small, floating ma and pa grocery store. Two very friendly and entrepreneurial residents of Road Town, out making the rounds. Mostly sweets and ice, but that's mostly what's needed. At least on *our* trips.

Life truly begins anew when you've soaked one of their brownies, approximately the size of first base, in Pusser's Rum, delivered straight to your transom in the middle of the Caribbean. Price is no object.

We tried all of this at home after our annual photo meeting, but somehow it just wasn't the same. Nonetheless, trip six ended on a high note. And Alan, at least, was beginning to talk about timing for next year.

7

BVI Revisited

No amount of skill, no equipment, and no boat will
keep you from disaster if you don't develop the most
important seagoing skill of all, a complete fear of
falling overboard.

—Lin and Larry Pardey

Our photo exchange meeting was in January so there was no
talk about wearing Buffett attire. We were all wearing ski
coats, which somehow elevated the anticipatory atmosphere.
A little pool, a little photo editing, a little whistle wetting, and a lot
of reminiscing.

We four, Alan, Beau, Oz and me, now thought of ourselves as
the four sailing musketeers. Flakey, Studly, Oz and Scout. We *were*
the trip. Accept no substitutes.

A planning meeting was scheduled for the next month. Freezing
temperatures may slow down the blood, but they speed up the
dreaming. You need to get the anticipation started when it's 20°F.

We began with a lot of enthusiasm, as always. Each of us put his
dream on the table. We mentioned all sorts of options like going to
Tonga or the Med, but no one pursued them. Little by little it became
apparent that as a group, we didn't want to mess with the formula.
Like a banana split: additions are okay, but no substitutions.

Talk began to center on a return to the Virgin Islands. No one
dared mention Tania. Deep in our hearts we knew we'd lost a lot of
the spirit of adventure, and settled into an easy routine. I finally
spoke my feelings.

"Look, I love the BVIs as much as the next guy," I said, almost
whining. "Good times or not, I sure as hell don't wanna go back

there. Exploration has given way to decadence. Comfort at least. I can't do it."

"That's way too harsh," observed Alan. "We had a super time last year. For Oz and me it was a great adventure. Was for you too, if you're honest about it."

"What's not to like about the BVIs?" asked Beau. "This whole thing's about having fun together, not some envelope-busting exercise."

"Jeez, Tom," pleaded Oz. "I don't think there's much to be gained with an ultimatum. We're only talking about next year. If Alan and Beau want to return, I'll go along and you should too. We'll do different anchorages, dive new spots, hike different islands. This is way too valuable to scrap."

Alan took up the baton. There was a certainty to his tone. "Damn right. The trip is the best thing I do all year. We started this together to be together. We've still got that, and we're still having fun."

"I actually had *more* fun last year," Beau added, a mock-seriousness to his voice. "We didn't have to spend half our time poring over charts trying to decide where we might find decent snorkeling or what reef to avoid."

Alan and Oz were willing to go along with almost anything, I remained more interested in discovery than vacationing, or at least vacationing that included discovery, and Beau, if he were pressed, didn't want me using the whole group to indulge my personal need for exploration. The objectives just weren't as easily congruent as they'd been six years earlier.

"Okay," I said, certain the resignation was clear in the body language. "I concede. I don't want to stop the carnival either." But we'd crossed a threshold. The big dreams seemed to have faded a bit into obscurity.

So we decided to return to the BVIs. They were completely compatible with what had seemingly become our kind of sailing. Close. Friendly. Predictable. Great restaurants. English deodorant. Caribbean rum. There *was* lots to like.

Going to the BVIs had the added virtue of good plane connections, so we lost less time. Less flying, more sailing. If you're gonna be cooped up together on a boat, may as well be near a beach, near decent food . . .

Yet after all this time we hadn't gotten used to the fact that when our plane passed over Orlando (it didn't, but hypothetically speaking), we were only half way there. Florida just seems a helluva long way from Colorado. Those Caribbean destinations were really *out there*. Certainly a complete disconnect from home. That still counted.

Oz and I went straight to Tortola, but Beau couldn't resist a day gambling in San Juan where he won nearly enough to pay for his trip. The dark side of his southern elegance.

Alan was again lost somewhere back in the States. Oz and I needed to creatively kill some time, and driving around like we'd done on Guadeloupe didn't grab us.

They have American-style cars there, but left side driving. The driver has to get *way* too far across the line to see if there's room to pass. Basically, you're side by side on some very hilly, curvy roads. More horrifying than a landing on Saba.

No horn was gonna protect us from near-certain death. "Two More Stupid Continentals Found Dead on Wrong Side of Road," the headline would read. Then Beau would *truly* never find us.

So we just hung out on the boat.

We completed checkout and were sitting there with a rum and tonic in contemplative moods. Rather quiet actually. Suddenly Oz looked over. "You know, the talk on these trips used to be about women and sports, mostly sports in my case. Have you noticed an increasing amount of shop talk sneaking in?"

I'd actually never heard that mild sort of disgust in his voice before. But I knew what he meant: way too many references to university stuff back home. "Damn right," I responded firmly. "I came down here to get away from all of it."

"Me too. Let's ban it," he said.

"Won't work."

"It will if it's costly enough. Could slow it down anyway. We've got to penalize that sort of misbehavior. It offends me." Hard to tell how serious he was.

"Lashes?" I suggested.

"Bligh's dead. Besides, I might slip up myself." He grinned.

"What about beer deprivation? Anyone who says something about work has to go all day without a drink."

"Not gonna work. Cookies, maybe."

"Hell, that would cause a mutiny."

The exchange continued. Out of these brilliant insights came a system of fines for prohibited stuff. We pulled out some napkins and a pen and put our creativity to work. It wasn't all that hard to identify *what* to ban. If we were going to honor the 75/25 norm of women and sports there just wasn't room for distracting conversation.

It was much more difficult to establish severity. Took us most of the evening, and not a few rum and tonics, heavy on lime juice, to get the scale right. In the end we decided that asking what time it is would cost a dollar, whining two dollars, and anything negative three. The heavy fines were saved for mentioning anyone or anything related to the university. For example, mentioning

a colleague	$ 5 each occurrence
the provost	$10
accreditation	$15
the dean	$25

We were naïve enough to think the pot might be empty at the end of the trip. Alas, the fines easily covered our expenses with DELIVERANCE. (Actually we agreed to give back $20 to anyone who puked, either out of sympathy or for its entertainment value, we're not sure; but in the BVIs no one did.)

Beau arrived the next evening, feeling flush with his gambling winnings. After a couple of hours we hit him with the "fine" monies he owed us. Made quite an ante. He thought it was such a genius idea he wasn't even mad about our not warning him.

We'd chartered a Privilege 42 catamaran to each have a separate room with an entire bed. Even with Beau sleeping diagonally, no complaints. No one stuck in the saloon. Two guys per head. Pure decadence.

The yacht was brand new, just arrived from France. We were to be the first charterers. Next day the three of us took it out for an hour (still no Alan), blew the port engine, and ended up spending a second night in the marina. Beautiful boat though, and it attracted attention.

About 5 p.m. that afternoon we were relaxing in our very spacious cockpit and noticed a young woman sort of drifting down the dock. 5'6" maybe. She was dressed in a tropical sarong-type wrap. Blue and green and aqua with some sort of white flower motif. Very smart though a bit faded. She had dish-watery blonde hair that came just below her shoulders, but looked like it could stand a good shampoo. Barefoot. She stopped right next to the transom and smiled, displaying a rather uneven set of large teeth. "How are you guys doing?"

"Never better. You?"

"Pretty good. Trying to get off this island for awhile, though. Where are you going?" She was looking straight at Beau, as most women did.

"Don't know yet. Just around the islands. We're waiting for another guy. Arrives tomorrow."

"Want some company?"

"Huh?"

"I can cook, clean. Most anything, really. Not looking for wages especially. Just need a change."

Whoa. She caught us a bit off guard. Three middle-aged professor types; this seemed highly unusual, at least to Oz and me. But we were still on our first rum and tonic at that point, and she was, well, visually challenging. Besides, we couldn't possibly keep it secret when we got home. So we passed, and she sort of drifted off down the dock. Deeply disappointed, we're certain.

(We second-guessed our decision that afternoon more than any we've ever made on these trips, but it was the right one: fantasy is almost always better than reality. And marriage, in our cases, is far better than the alternative.)

We talked about "the girl" for quite awhile. Later we taxied over to Cane Garden Bay to make sure Rhymer's hadn't forgotten us. On the way over we swung by the Bomba Shack, a ramshackle institution on the north side of Tortola festooned with T-shirts, bras and panties. It's even more colorfully and completely decorated than Rhymer's and its neighbors in Cane Garden.

The Bomba is famous for its monthly Full Moon parties where, if you can hold on long enough, nudity becomes the norm. That's what we were told anyway. We read a bunch of the tributes scrawled on the walls (there are hundreds, most of which cannot be repeated), had a beer and left with our clothes on. The sun was still up.

Initially we intended to anchor at Cane Garden, as we'd done last year, and wait for Alan (he'd made another set of CDs), but the blown engine and rough northerlies took care of that. So we picked him up at Fat Hog Bay the next day.

Oz took the lead. "You wouldn't believe what happened to us at the marina yesterday."

"Probably not," said Alan, intensely interested, as always.

"Blown engine." Oz had adopted a beautifully appropriate blasé tone.

"No kidding?"

"Gets better. A girl stopped by and offered to join us."

Alan's eyes grew and he glanced inside the cabin. "So where is she?"

"Turned her down."

"Impossible."

"Gorgeous thing. Maybe 22, 23. Great body too. Said she was willing to do anything."

"You're kidding." Alan was barely able to contain himself.

"Only on the gorgeous part. Actually she was too ugly."

"Impossible."

"And she didn't seem to have offsetting virtues."

"Impossible."

"Good thing you weren't there to vote." Oz turned away, never changing his expression. Then gave Beau and me a huge grin. We responded with grins of our own and a quick thumbs up.

Alan found the subject hard to abandon, eventually questioning our sanity. But the weather gods were beginning to cooperate so we raised the sails and shot around West End over to Jost Van Dyke.

Foxy's Tamarind Bar and Grill in Great Harbour is a BVI institution. It's quantum leaps beyond the typical Caribbean beachside dive. It looks to have been built with greater care, one section at a time, so it has several open-air rooms; and it has booths.

Especially, Foxy's has permanence—and tradition. Among the rafters of T-shirts are sailing burgees, football jerseys, hats, pictures, you name it. Signed paper currency from all over the world stapled to the beams. Out on the beach, a beautiful hammock strung between two palms.

So we decided to take the dinghy in for dinner, one of our favorite ways to avoid doing dishes. We declared it a "crew shirt" occasion. Looked downright elegant.

Oz steered the dinghy to the beach, saying he needed the practice. Got within 15 feet of shore when—and it all occurred in an instant—Oz rotated the grip the wrong way, gunning the motor, while also swinging the handle the wrong way. We went broadside to a wave of maybe eighteen inches and capsized. Completely soaked in about two feet of very sandy salt water. The audience of ten or so laughed, shot a few pictures, even pointed at us.

Beau jumped up and stated, just a bit too loudly, "I have returned, as promised."

Alan looked at Oz. "Did Beau pay you to create a MacArthur moment for him?"

"Seems more reminiscent of Normandy," I said as though I'd been there.

"Are we claiming this island?" Alan asked, looking around blankly.

"I left the flag on the boat," I responded. "Sorry."

"Somehow," noted Alan, still surveying the situation, "I didn't think a peacetime landing would be this messy. The only thing dry is my hat."

"Well, you look like you've been through a car wash on your ski rack," I said. "Where's the brush?"

All during this exchange Oz was downright obsequious with his endless apologies for doing it backwards.

"I still feel like ol' Mac," Beau stated solemnly. He'd stretched himself up to his full 6'6" presence. It appeared he thought that with enough grandeur no one would notice we'd looked like a local fisherman emptying his tub on a market table.

"Personally," I said casually to Oz, "I'm suing you. It's not just the shirt and my camera. It's the indignity."

"Screw dignity," mumbled Alan, who looked surprisingly normal dripping wet. "What this really means, Oz, is that you're doing all the dishes from now on."

Oz kept apologizing.

"If true," I said, "it was worth it. But we're still dining out. Let's loop back and put on something dry."

"Nah," said Beau sarcastically. "I think we ought to go to dinner like we are. Mac would've."

"Get back in the boat, Douglas," suggested Alan. "The cameras are off. Media's gone home."

"Compromise," I offered firmly. "Only Oz goes to dinner like he is. We might run into some of those same people. The rest of us could engage in some serious finger-pointing."

Thinking I might actually be serious, Oz agreed to that. So we knocked him down again, then went back to the yacht and cleaned up. All of us. This time Alan drove.

Foxy's was worth the delay. It smelled of charcoal and grease and coconuts. Fine food too. Plus it has Foxy, who is no mean entertainer. We chatted with him awhile, had burgers and beers. Shot some pictures that are among our favorites since, prior to tripping the shutter, we poured beer over Oz's head to ease his guilt and remember the landing.

Next day we were flying east at maybe eight knots; I was at the helm. The other three were arranged on the bow seats and tramp, headsets on, blasting great, personalized music into their heads. They were all singing, presumably the tune each had on his CD at the time. Clearly all different. Lots of body movement too. Right out of *One Flew Over the Cuckoo's Nest* from my vantage point.

Beau dropped his koozie overboard and Oz ran the length of the boat to retrieve it from the swim platform before we passed it. Unfortunately the boat hook missed, Oz lost his footing and fell in.

We had practiced this. Well, at least we'd talked about it. Alas, nothing floatable was even remotely within reach. I shouted "Man overboard!" and began turning the cat. The other two guys jumped up, raced back and grabbed—the life ring? Not a chance: they shot below and grabbed their cameras. We create memories.

Oz, a big guy and very buoyant, was rapidly getting smaller in the wake. But in the flat seas we were back in a hurry and picked him up.

"Gawd," he panted, "I thought for a minute you guys were just gonna sail off. Wasn't sure how long I could last back there. Gets lonely in a hurry."

"Glad you stayed afloat," I said, tossing him a towel. "Had a short delay in getting some help. We're not exactly ready to be the Coast Guard training film. Time we got ready to toss the ring it'd been further away than the boat."

Beau and Alan were laughing now, and ready to defend themselves. "Hell, we got back here in record time." . . . "The back-winded jib impeded our progress." . . . "With all that body fat we knew you'd be fine." . . . "Good thing a whale didn't come by and try to mate" . . . "I'll get you a beer. Looks like you've already got a koozie." . . . "We got some great pictures."

I was never happier not to be the guy in the water. Oz now knows who his friends are. And the photos stunk.

Next day we hit The Baths, the stretch of Virgin Gorda that served, so legend goes, as bathtubs for pirates. Gigantic granite boulders that form calm pools, shafts of light filtering between them. People crawl all over them, and swim among them. They are very picturesque, on the cover of every brochure. No visit to the BVIs is complete without going to The Baths. Anchor off fifty meters and swim in.

We paid our usual respects, but this day a swell made it uncomfortable. To make matters worse, Oz got stung by a jellyfish on the way in, raising an ugly welt across his shoulder and chest. We shot the mandatory pictures, expressed passing sympathy ("Nasty birthmark, Oz," "Try less follow-through on your forehand," etc.), and left early.

We picked up a mooring at Cooper Island where last year we'd run into that other crew from Colorado. It was still early in the day, so we went ashore and paid the mooring fee. Moorings are scarce at Cooper Island and anchoring is difficult on the grassy bottom.

In my pre-guys-trip days I'd once spent an entire night in the cockpit without sleep to make sure my boat wasn't dragging. Not the sort of adventure I wanted to repeat. Particularly with a crew who would be content to sleep through the whole thing. Sleep was right up there with big limes and great cigars.

So we rented a mooring, tied our dinghy to it and went sailing. Several hours later we returned to find another yacht tied to it too. We came alongside.

"Ah, that's our mooring," I yelled, in a yachty-friendly way.

"Don't think so," came the response. "We're obviously on it."

There were three couples on board, all lined up along the rail of a white-hulled 42-foot rent-a-yacht. The guy talking was clearly speaking for them all.

"Yeah, but we paid for it." My volume level was increasing.

"Leave it, you lose it."

"We tied our dinghy to it."

"So? We're on this mooring. You're not." A couple of them actually smiled.

"Well, get the hell off." I was shouting now, likely with more than a little edge to the demand. We had lots of onlookers: the anchorage at Cooper Island is an intimate place. Beau saved me from further useless embarrassment.

"Look," he yelled nicely to them. "Just do the right thing. Leave the mooring. We rented it. We have a receipt. We're happy to show it to you. Or call the Beach Club on the VHF and ask 'em. Do the right thing. We'll wait."

They huddled, and five minutes later they dropped the line and left to go try anchoring. As fate would have it they had the table next to us at the Beach Club for dinner. As always, Beau had them all laughing in a matter of minutes. You'd have thought he was part of their crew. I don't know how he does it.

That night we sat in the cockpit and stared at the lights of Tortola, a few miles away, against an ebony sky. It was one of the Caribbean's most memorable scenes. We did a few *If* questions, but we made 'em up, stuff like "What music would you want at your wake?" Or, "If you had to, what food could you eat every day?" We weren't as creative as the book.

Next day the weather was squally. But the winds were huge so we took off to go sailing again. If anyone was gonna get the puke reward, this would have been the time.

A 4- to 5-foot chop made the cat hobby horse at lot. But Alan and Oz were on the bow seats, white-knuckling the pulpit railings, soaked from the waves and rain. Whooping it up, laughing like hell. Beau and I were aft. Not bouncing as much, but just as wet.

We ended up at The Indians mid-afternoon to do some snorkeling. No one else was there since the rain had driven the smart ones into The Bight on Norman Island. We picked up a day mooring.

Alan and Beau decided to stay aboard to debate, over a beverage no doubt, whether they could cast out far enough to fish legally. (No dice.) Oz and I jumped in to check out the fish life. It's excellent there: almost as good as we'd had off Guadeloupe. The Sergeant Majors and Yellowtails, especially, swarmed all over you, expecting to be fed.

Maybe twenty minutes later we looked up and noticed the cat was on a different mooring. We swam over.

"Just curious," I asked, "why did you change moorings?"

Alan grinned. "Mooring line broke."

"You're kidding. Those things are maintained by the government."

"We're in da islands, mon." He held it up. "Good thing Beau was paying attention."

"Good thing we weren't all snorkeling," I said seriously.

"Good point."

Our discussions that evening focused on various "what if" scenarios related to experiences at The Indians. Scary stuff. "Long distance swimming" was an oft-mentioned phrase: the nearest boat at Norman Island had been nearly a mile away. And the next stop for a half million dollar catamaran (owned by someone a whole lot richer than we are) might have been St. Croix. Now that's *really* a long way off.

Fortunately this long, very long, period of reflection, fear and laughter was made easier by the return of DELIVERANCE. Brownies and Pusser's never tasted so good. We put a double loop on the mooring in The Bight before doing some Dave Barry and calling it a night. We'd already done enough *If* questions.

The next morning was an exhilarating, but quiet, sail back to the marina. Didn't even seem to be much conversation on the way back to the airport, at least not the sort of animated chatter we'd had before. It felt like the guys were really ready to go home.

There was plenty of adventure on this trip, but we didn't go after much of it. It just seemed to find us. I'm not sure what Tania would think.

At our post-trip photo meeting we did not set a date to talk about next year. That was a first, and it was a sign.

8

Trips of a Different Sort

The ocean has always been a salve to my soul . . .
the best thing for a cut or abrasion was to go swimming in salt water. Later down the road of life, I made
the discovery that salt water was also good for the
mental abrasions one inevitably acquires on land.

—Jimmy Buffett

We did take a year off sailing but still found a reason to get together. We went to see a rodeo of "Bull Riders Only" in Las Vegas. All five trip veterans; five because George seemed permanently gone. We hope that, wherever he is, he's dressed.

We weren't sailing, but it was a hoot. Oz and Beau love small stakes gambling, Darren's a huge rodeo fan (his boots looked normal there), and Alan and I didn't want to miss any of the fun. Poolside viewing was excellent.

The workers at the tables know a fish when they see him: I lost $50 in less than ten minutes and went back to the pool. Gotta do what you're good at.

We took a day off from the casinos and rodeo to tour the town. We found a track not far away where we could race go-carts. That set up some rather lively competition.

Beau lost three straight races and was disgusted. He wasn't used to losing at anything. "I've got a slow car."

That prompted the usual warm, understanding group responses. "The problem is you create too much wind resistance." . . . "Lighter is quicker." . . . "Your knees are bent so far up they're blocking your vision." . . . "Your reflexes are deader than Tania's motor."

"Hell, Tania's motor is in my car."

"Quit whining. The cars are all the same."

"Impossible. I keep losing."

"Fine. Let's rotate cars."

We did. He still lost. We laughed like hell.

On the way back to town we passed one of those multi-story anti-gravity towers. An expensive vertical thrill ride. As usual Beau was driving since he always pleaded leg space. Alan wanted him to stop.

"No chance," said Beau. "It's beneath my dignity to go up in one of those."

"You're still pissed off because you didn't win, aren't you?" asked Alan. "Not stopping just for spite. You don't have to go and look stupid. Just stop."

"Actually," countered Beau, "we're saving you from yourself. Your proclivity to barf cannot be overestimated."

"*If*," Alan asked expansively, "you knew you were going to die tomorrow, wouldn't you want to experience everything legal and available?"

I sighed. "Just because you left the book at home, Alan, doesn't mean you can invent questions. Besides, it's early and we've got no port."

We were a couple of blocks away by this time, and Oz had been mostly looking out the window. He surprised us by turning toward Alan in the back seat. "Think of us as your guardians. We're saving you from one more public humiliation."

"I don't need you guys," Alan said defensively. "Never have."

"Crap," I said. "Without us, you don't get out of town. Poolside attractions are summoning."

That seemed to satisfy him. The last mile or so to the hotel passed in silence since no one was sure who won the last few rounds, though Beau clearly had one in each of the W-L columns. In any case he managed to win plenty at the tables and have the last laugh. Maybe his size was intimidating.

The highlight of the rodeo was to be on the last night. Terry Don West, the greatest bull rider in the world, was going to ride Bodacious, the meanest bull in the world, in an exhibition. Bodacious had an unequalled reputation for violence: no one had ever successfully ridden him for the mandatory eight seconds.

West had been thrown onto his head and face the night before, however. Spent the night in the hospital and was not expected to appear.

But when the time came, there he was, mounting up in the chute, wearing what looked to be a lacrosse helmet, complete with face guard.

The chute opened, and out came this gigantic raging animal. Dark brownish black. Snorting, twisting, bucking. He was *huge* and he was *furious* about having someone perched on his back. That cinch probably didn't help his disposition either.

West gave him a ride unlike anything we, and apparently the audience, had ever seen. Eight agonizing seconds of uncontrolled violence. West hung on. The crowd went nuts.

When it was over, Terry Bradshaw, doing the TV commentary, rushed out to interview him. He was a full head taller than West. And he was not wearing a cowboy hat on that very distinctive Bradshaw head. Quite reflective, actually.

"No one expected you to be here tonight. Why'd you come out here and risk your life?"

"These people came heah expectin' it," he said in his Oklahoma drawl. "Had to."

"Man, you're crazier than a football player," said Bradshaw with that tone of disbelief he seems to have mastered.

West looked right up at him. Never cracked a smile. "Smaller too."

I think even a New Jersey girl like Tania would have understood that level of courage.

Of course we rode the roller coaster at New York New York, watched the sea battle at Treasure Island, and were enchanted by the water fountain show at the Bellagio. But the best part was being back together.

Even without limes, visors, crew shirts or CDs, we managed to pick up right where we'd left off. We didn't do much philosophizing (maybe we needed a break), yet the jokes, the ribbing, and the conversations about women and sports didn't miss a beat.

But in the end Vegas wasn't our cup of tea. Too many lights. Very little salt water.

* * *

The next year Alan and I somehow got invited to help deliver a boat through the Oswego and Erie Canals, down the Hudson River and into the Chesapeake. Normally this might smack of too much work and too few bikinis, but we signed on. Alan went because he'd go anywhere out of state to sail. I joined for the education: new places, new challenges, new people.

Locks were a new phenomenon. I was fascinated by these simple engineering miracles, built 175 years earlier, which allowed boats, the only reliable transportation at the time, to link commerce between the East Coast and the Midwest via the Great Lakes.

They seem anachronistic now. When we traversed these 23 locks, we were, often as not, the only boat in them. That didn't seem to reduce any of the yelling on board however. Looking back, it seems the amount of shouting was inversely proportional to the number of other boats in the lock.

The mast had been horizontal during the entire run down the canals. It was all bundled up and lashed to elaborate sets of temporary gallows. Scaffolding apparently built by blind men (before we got aboard) on the bow and stern. At least twenty 2x4s and duct tape in quantities resembling misshapen sharks. Another jury rig constructed amidships to assure banging one's head when emerging from the companionway. Every time.

With the mast down one of our early stops was to pull in and get it re-stepped.

"Ever done this before?" I asked Alan.

"Nope," he responded. "Matter of fact, I've never seen a horizontal mast."

"Me either. Think we're gonna be any help?"

"Not a chance," he suggested.

And in fact, we weren't. We tried to look knowledgeable when the crane hoisted the stick to vertical. We even plugged in a few wires and did our best to assist in the tensioning of the shrouds.

But mostly we did what we'd become expert at, at moments like these: look on approvingly while sipping a beer. We even had cigars to appear more nonchalant. The marina guys didn't call on us for help, but we're sure they knew we were right there on standby.

A couple of beers later we took off; no sail, but at least we looked like a yacht again and we were moving. The little towns along the canals and the upper Hudson are charming.

As one gets nearer to New York City, the hills are lined with enormous houses, barely visible among the dense growth of deciduous trees. Very old money, lots of it. Almost expected to catch a fleeting glance of Ichabod Crane riding among them.

"Look up to the right," said the skipper, pointing. "There's West Point."

West Point, from the water, has the stark look of something medieval. Gray, angular, windowless from our vantage point. It was constructed on the river bend as just that: a strategic point with a commanding view of the Hudson in both directions. It's on the west side, of course, but it had somehow never occurred to me the name had geographical, as well as military, significance.

"Sure is stark and ominous," I offered, just trying to make small talk.

"Well, it was originally a fort," he said knowledgeably.

"Looks more like a prison. No escape," I thought aloud. One large lobster trap.

He looked back to the water ahead. "Yeah. Bet those guys wish they were down here." Our skipper was an Annapolis grad.

"Probably," I agreed. "They'd have felt right at home when we were going through the locks." The skipper didn't seem to get the jab, but then he hadn't been on the guys' trips to cultivate his sarcasm gene.

Still, we really did feel fortunate. And we were fortunate too that Jim Currier, a well-known writer of sailing books and articles, was also aboard. Not only did he have lots of great stories, he had called Pete Seeger, one of America's greatest folksingers, because he wanted to interview him.

Seeger lives in a tiny little town on the Hudson. (We'll protect the precise location from invasion.) He had invited Currier to stop in. We came along as baggage. Tied up at a rickety dock.

There was a small yellow notice tacked to the boathouse door announcing a corn fest the following weekend. The sign proclaimed free boat rides, crafts and food. In letters so tiny one would hardly notice, it also said, "Free Entertainment with David Crosby and Pete Seeger." Just your average weekend corn fest duo.

Seeger met us there, banjo in hand. He played and sang a couple of songs. We felt really special to have this private audience. It was a truly historic moment for each of us, though I'm not sure Currier ever got his interview.

Besides Pete the most memorable part of this side trip was that the town not only had Seeger, it had the most voracious chiggers known to man. There were hundreds of those blood-hungry mites. Maybe they're attracted by folk singing.

I was sleeping in the V-bunk. The hatch overhead seemed to act like a giant vacuum, drawing those chiggers right into my space. Next day I looked like a smallpox victim.

Doctor visits, prescription filling (just what you want to do on a New York City layover), and the most insatiable desire to scratch. It lasted for days.

We overnighted on the Jersey shore across from Manhattan. A visit to Ellis Island reminded us we were just one more boatload of immigrants, albeit one from the west, to pass that way. With boxes of tape instead of family heirlooms. If I hadn't been scratching so damn much I'd have enjoyed it even more. All those names. So much history.

In the Chesapeake we visited St. Michaels on the eastern shore, a quaint little village Beau and Oz would have loved. America's equivalent of Terre de Haut off Guadeloupe. Incredible seafood. No tropics, but so much charm even crème brûlée wasn't necessary.

Alan and I both got what we came for, and we had a few drinks and shared some lies, not to mention cigars. But it was only about a "6" on the fun scale. Too much motoring and too little sailing. Mostly, though, we missed *our* crew. We would never have considered *If* questions with these guys.

It was, however, thoroughly inspirational: Manhattan skyline, Miss Liberty. You got to do it once, like seeing the Red Sox play in Fenway.

9

The Bahamas

The tradition nearly died out. I felt pretty sure the whole idea had run its course. But Alan, still looking for an escape, bounded into my office not long after the delivery. A stack of large cookies in one hand. Oatmeal, probably. Same sandals and khakis, I think, but he was wearing a "crew shirt." Had to be on purpose.

He was grinning from ear to ear, waiving one of those big cookies. He almost shouted, "We gotta have a reunion."

"I don't think so, Alan. I love you guys, but we're all doing different stuff these days."

"It's been a coupla years," he gushed. "We'll bring back all the traditions. Go someplace new. It'd be a blast."

"I don't know. The memories are terrific. Let's let them be."

Alan was not giving up. "We just let things wind down, that's all. We gotta go out, if we're going out, with a *bang*. A guys' trip reunion."

"Finale?"

"That's your term. Mine's reunion. We'll celebrate ten years of sailing." He was just so *exuberant*. Cookie crumbs were flying everywhere.

"Okay. Check with Beau and Oz. See what they think."

He bolted from the office and was back in less than an hour. "They're in! When do you want to meet?"

We did meet the following week to plan the reunion: something to properly celebrate a decade of sailing. Or a decade of decadence. Or maybe we really did just miss getting away for a real "guys' trip." In any case, we missed the crew meetings: they were half the fun.

All of us, Beau, Oz, Alan and I wore a crew shirt (we each owned a drawer of them: the selection was limitless) and met again over charts and rum and tonics. We invited Darren, but I think his boots were in the shop. Maybe he was back in Siberia; maybe we embarrassed him with our Nikes at the rodeo.

True to form, Alan brought new visors. Our old ones were really sweat-stained by now, which actually made them *more* attractive to us, but you just couldn't wear them in mixed company any longer. It was even a little questionable on the golf course.

More importantly they were completely covered with tender messages. No more room to write fuzzy stuff like, "Puke King," "The mission is voyage, not voyeur." "Next time grab the life ring on your way off the boat." "I never liked the logo." "DELIVERANCE or death." "Spinnaker Stud." "Peas are beautiful." "Peas *still* suck."

Amidst all those stains, some of these endearments had become hard to read, but we knew they were there. Ready for bronzing.

The four of us embarked upon our usual hours of debate about locations and boats, frequently interrupted by some incredible story from the past. One of the very few meetings I didn't want to stop. The sense of adventure may have waned, but the "guy spirit" was definitely back.

There wasn't any talk this time about returning to the BVIs. We'd been there twice. Not much debate about returning to *any* of our former sailing grounds, actually. We needed new memories. And we had a lot of personal objectives to meet if we were going to "go out with a bang:" escape, exploration, relaxation, some challenge but not too much, and lots of "guy time."

Alan knew he was the catalyst and jumped right in. "Let's go to Martinique. Not that hard to reach. Beautiful place, I've heard. Good anchorages. Foreign. Exotic."

"Alan, you're pathetically transparent," groaned Beau. "All you really care about is looking at naked French women."

"I just happen to love the female form."

"I used to love breasts too," I said. " 'Till I grew my own."

We all laughed and it felt good. These were friends who no longer had any pretenses, and damn few secrets. All those *If* questions had caused one helluva lot of revelation. Ten years of sharing runs deep.

In the end we opted for the Abacos as none of us had experienced the Bahamas. And the Bahamas had not experienced us. Plus they had a cat, an Athena 38.

Aside from the bed space (we were back to three cabins and a short straw), this was our most civilized trip. Perhaps we were better sailors. Perhaps we were just older. The cigars were more expensive, and so was the port. They, the company, and the wonderful Bahamian people made it all worthwhile. Determined to make this trip special, Alan created all new CDs.

We had, however, become concerned about the availability of diet tonic in the Bahamas, a condition made necessary by our tendency to gain ten pounds on each trip. Our charter company said it was not available (What kind of a question is that?), so we investigated shipping a case down there.

It cost about twenty times as much to ship as it cost to buy, unless it went by "ground and boat." Figured we'd be dead by then; might have gotten tied up in some remote customs office too.

So we decided on a dedicated piece of tonic luggage. Weighed 40 lbs. We had to rotate who dragged it. Customs at Marsh Harbor was also very interesting.

This large, very large, uniformed customs officer was rummaging through our bags at random. Some of them he just waived through; some he asked us to open. He got to the misshapen heavy one. "Wha's in da bag?"

"Diet tonic," I answered in my most respectful voice. Even a ninny wouldn't want to irritate anyone from customs or immigration, especially in a new country.

"Wha's dat?"

"Tonic. Stuff you mix with rum. Or gin. Like gin and tonic." I smiled.

"Oh, lie quinine watta. We already got dat heah."

"Not like this. It's sugar-free."

"Why you wahn dat?"

He seemed to suspect we were importers, we had so much of it. But in the end, he gave us one of those warm Bahamian smiles and wished us well.

"Go hah fun on da boat. Puh plenny o' tonic in dem drings. Deh's lossa crazy pursuns frum de mainland' ow dah. Doan wanna be no in-tox-i-cated." We invited him to stop by for a drink. Sugar free. He just kept smiling, waving us through.

We boarded the boat and checked out without incident. The Bahamians were not only friendly, they smelled good. Everything smelled good. The aroma of gardenias was pervasive. Gardenias and salt water. No one said it, but we were all thinking we should have done this place years earlier. Quite a contrast to some of our Caribbean experiences. Especially the boat checkout.

Before the Virgin Island trips we'd never have a phone aboard. Emergencies were far lower on the priority list than escape. In the BVIs we ordered one, but we never told anyone. Certainly didn't want that thing to ring. Selective outgoing calls only. All of them by Oz.

Over the years Oz had become increasingly guilty about being away from his two young daughters for a whole week. Felt a compelling need to call home nightly. We noticed, however, he was also getting sports scores from his wife. $4 a minute plus hookup charges.

This provided the rest of us a great opportunity to fill up our glasses, head for the trampoline, and create a betting pool: how big his phone bill would be. Those kids talked more every year.

The procedure was for the other three of us to each secretly write a number on a napkin, $20 entry. Right off Alan asked, "What were his bills in the BVIs?"

Trip expenses were part of the camp counselor's job, so I responded, "Not sure. Maybe $150 the first year. Over two hundred last time."

"Ya gotta be kidding."

"Nope. More'n I'd personally give the phone company. Rum's a better deal. Three bucks a fifth and before long you can't find the phone even if you wanted to."

"It'd make me *feel* better too." Alan was slouched across the tramp. Didn't look like *anything* could make him feel any better.

"Agreed," I responded. "But whatta we know? We don't have kids."

Beau, who'd been contemplating his bid, joined in. "I do. Seems to me though, that some separation is good. Creates independence. No calls, in or out. Un-find-a-ble: *I'm* certainly enjoying it."

I smiled. "Damn, Beau. You've become as cynical as George."

"Ah, George. May he be happy among deaf nudists."

We each wrote down our estimate. Whoever made the highest guess always won. In the Bahamas the actual tab was, trust me, nearly $400. And the Bahamas are *way* closer than the BVIs. Duty-free made a killing when we left.

Besides the phone we had a GPS for the first time on this trip. Good thing. There are lots of places in the Abacos with very skinny water. Sure they're well marked on the charts, but without putting a bunch of waypoints into the GPS, we might have grounded a few times, even with a cat. Besides, the GPS provided a weird form of entertainment for the three of us while Oz ran up his phone bill. The first night at anchor was particularly entertaining.

"Is north at the top?"

"I don't think so. I think it's the way we're headed."

"How do you know where north is?"

"Doesn't matter. Only matters where you are and where you want to be."

"I'd feel better if I knew where north is."

"I'll feel better if we don't ground this boat."

We were, for a while, very steep on the GPS learning curve.

One of the other things we learned is that cookie shortages are not restricted to the Caribbean. We ran out, as usual, on Day Three. Hope Town saved us.

Hope Town is, excuse the non-guy talk, the cutest place we'd ever seen. Twisty, narrow streets lined with little clapboard houses painted in pastels: pink, yellow, baby blue, pistachio, lavender, mauve(?), tangerine (if one has an expanded color palette). Like snorkeling at Cousteau Underwater Park.

Each one trimmed in white, with a red metal roof. Nearly all had small signs out front with some descriptive note in print or flowing script. Things like, "Jenny's B&B," "Jim & Suzie Wilson," "Maude Jones, Seamstress."

Hope Town also has this stately, candy-striped lighthouse, which can be seen for miles in the Abacos. It's open to the public, and it's essential to climb up to the platform at the top. The view is breathtaking. From there the little houses are a Monet.

It was on the descent from the lighthouse that Alan suggested we'd better load up on cookies. After a climb like that, a guy just can't get enough cookies. Fortunately ample supplies existed in Hope Town, even if the selection was weak. Inside the market the lights stayed on. Not only that, there were large limes in abundance. No reunion scurvy.

The only odd part of Hope Town was an old clapboard house right next to the market. Completely weathered wood. All the windows boarded over. Must have been a dozen cats roaming the open crawl space underneath, and lying on the porch.

We'd asked the store clerk about it and she told us the "Cat Lady" lived there alone, except for her animals. "She liv in de dark," the girl offered. "Say nuttin' to no-bod-y. Sum-ti' we pass 'long ol' food."

When we came back out, there she was, sitting quietly on the porch stoop among the cats. She was dirty and poorly dressed. She was clearly the *other* side of Hope Town life.

No one said a word on our way back to the boat. We lounged around the cockpit for several minutes in reflective moods. It took us some large rum and tonics to talk about the contrasts.

"Not all gardenias in the Bahamas," observed Oz.

"Pretty sad," Alan responded. "But she seemed serene. Almost content."

Beau got philosophical. "Reminds me a bit of Coconut Johnny. Satisfied with himself. Peaceful."

"Sure hope so," I added. "It'd be just too ironic to have genuine misery in a place this idyllic."

"Is it we who are fortunate?" asked Oz. "Or her?"

"We may need more time than we've got," I answered, "to figure that one out."

Next morning Alan, Oz and I were collected in the cockpit. "Where to next?" I asked them, an apple in one hand, steaming mug of coffee in the other. They were having cookies and milk, their usual breakfast unless someone got out cereals or some potato chips.

"Doesn't matter now," said Alan, "since our larder is re-supplied." His favorite was a half bag of Oreos to jump-start the day. He ate them in two bites, without pulling them apart and licking out the white part. But he still waved them around for emphasis when making a point.

"Wherever the wind blows us," offered Oz, who was working on his own bag of Chips Ahoy.

Beau emerged from the companionway with a bowl of something healthy-looking, sliced bananas on top, and a can of juice in his other hand. Then he went back to retrieve his coffee, a spoon and a napkin. "I don't care much either," he said. "But let's not rush outta here. I'd like a settled stomach."

"You wouldn't have that problem," suggested Alan, "if you'd put the right things in it."

"Sometimes," Beau responded, "your creative approach to life deserves to be ignored. Second, cookies and juice are a lousy combination. Third, you have a well-deserved reputation as the barf king of this crew. Maybe it's your diet."

"Maybe," said Alan. "But all that juice seems to be giving you an attitude."

"You love me and you know it," responded Beau. "Let's just eat in peace."

"Okay. Long as I don't have to do your dishes."

About ten we unhooked from the mooring and took off. Next stop was Man-o-War Cay, a lot more tranquil than the name suggests. Tiny community where nearly everyone has the same last name. Charming, but there's nothing much there except several boat building places, a gift shop or two. We visited on a Sunday and everything was closed up tight as a casket. Very religious residents.

Probably just as well: in addition to being religious, it's dry, so we wouldn't have hung around long anyway.

On our way south we picked up a day mooring at Sandy Cay to do some snorkeling. Alan and Beau took off in one direction, Oz and I in another. Not five minutes later, Oz tapped my shoulder. We both popped our heads up, pulled out our snorkels.

Oz's eyes were huge behind his mask. His body was motionless. Rigid almost. All the animation was in his voice. "Do you see *that*?" He was pointing down through about 10 feet of water to a sand shark. Maybe 6-7 feet long.

"Yeah. Pretty cool, huh? But this camera won't shoot that far down. I'm going to see how far down I can dive."

"Are you nuts? It's a SHARK."

"Well sure. But it's only a sand shark. Pretty harmless. Besides, it's asleep."

"If you wake it up it will not be harmless," Oz said with growing alarm. "Don't you watch PBS? *Nothing* is harmless jerked up in the middle of a nap. It will be *pissed*."

"I'm not gonna wake it," I responded. "I'm just gonna shoot a picture."

"Why don't you just tap its nose and ask for a pose? I'm *outta* here."

And with that, all those body parts leaped into motion. Oz headed toward the boat at a speed that almost resulted in levitation. He was off that swim platform faster'n I'd have thought possible for a man of his size. Sort of *launched* out of the water like a missile, right into the cockpit. Water flying off his body. Still wearing his mask and fins.

The shark never moved. In my photo it's not even visible.

We sailed a lot in those skinny Bahamian waters, grateful for our GPS. And we anchored in some sublime little spots. One of our favorites was Little Harbour. A pod of dolphins on our starboard bow accompanied us through the narrow entrance.

Once inside, the bay is nearly circular. On the east shore is Johnson's Studio which seemed to offer paintings and sculpture. It was closed when we visited, however. But Pete's Pub next door was definitely open.

Pete's looks like a small version of the Bomba Shack. You'd swear a stiff breeze would blow it away, but it seems to have survived everything. More than slightly shopworn though.

Several other sailors were sitting around nursing beers. Most of them looked liked they'd been adrift for months: week-old beards, bad hair, stained T-shirts, leathered skin. They must have been enjoying their cruises.

We joined 'em of course, exchanging sailing stories of one sort or another. Finding out home towns, occupations. The usual stuff. The beers were cold and the cigars were a hit. But the food appeared a bit suspect, so we dinghied back to our boat for dinner.

Beau's cooking hadn't missed a beat. Maybe his culinary creativity had actually improved.

This yacht had an astonishing inventory of cooking equipment, plates, cutlery. Beau had, early on, opened and closed all the drawers, examining their contents.

"Great galley," he said with pleasure.

"Depends who you ask," I responded. "Seems excessive."

He was still lost in his discovery process. "This may be the first time I never lacked for tools of the trade."

"Think you'll find a way to employ them all?"

"No problem," he said soothingly, never looking up. "It's all here to be used."

"Daily?"

We got to know every piece. Intimately.

After washing dinner dishes there seemed precious little time for poker, *If* and Dave Barry readings, but they were essential trip components, so we squeezed them in. We had no trouble fitting in the cigars and port.

Alan had actually been on time for this trip, so of course he had to leave early. Booked himself on the ferry from Hope Town. We returned there, dropped him off a half hour early, eased out of the harbor and anchored. Then we three productively spent the time figuring out how to embarrass him when the ferry came by.

"How about water balloons?" We'd learned to pack emergency supplies.

"Can't get 'em ready in time. Ferry will be out in a few minutes."

"Radio her, say there's an emergency and it must return to the dock."

"Illegal for sure. Let's not see the inside of a Bahamian jail."

"How 'bout we stand here with linked arms, totally naked."

"Gawd, is George here?"

"How about a moon?"

"You gotta be kidding. I haven't done that since I had a butt I *wanted* to show."

"All our butts look alike: bone white and ugly."

"Three of them ought to make quite a sight."

"Illegal for sure. These people are as modest as Mom."

In the end we just couldn't seem to stop ourselves from indulging in one last enduring act of adolescence. So we took off our shirts and loosened our trunks. When the boat got directly abeam, and Alan was waving and shouting he'd see us back home, we did elegant pirouettes, bent over and tri-mooned him and a ferry full of local commuters, most of whom ignored us. Well, we think they ignored us: our sight lines were impaired.

Perhaps it provided a fitting bookend for these trips: we'd sort of started with nudity too. Sometimes even middle-aged men do stupid things. Maybe often.

That night the three of us took some of the edge off our feelings of remorse by once again sitting out on the trampoline, staring up at the stars, with port and cigars. We watched a moonrise so astonishing we could only stare. It was huge. Full. Bright orange.

The salt air felt almost melancholy with the odyssey coming to a close. It was overwhelmingly silent. No one suggested pulling out Dave Barry or the *If* book: didn't seem right without Alan.

"I'll miss the guy," Oz suddenly reflected.

"Don't go sentimental on us, Oz," Beau suggested, not moving his eyes from the amazing sky.

"Okay, he's a flaky artist," I observed. "But ya gotta love him."

Beau laughed. "Hell, we all do. The drummer he's marching to is playing bongos."

"Still seems weird without him," said Oz.

"Amen" said Beau. "But we'll see him in Colorado in a coupla days."

"I feel a bit like Oz," I mused, still looking straight up. "Alan could be twenty better than any of us." I couldn't see it in the dark, but I know all three of us were grinning.

Alan was, after all, the catalyst for all of this. He alone, perhaps, understood from the beginning the real purpose was more escape than adventure. Cast off the dock lines and just *go*. The rest will take care of itself. Discovery, in the end, was as much about ourselves and each other as it was about places.

The four of us still get together a couple of times a year, for a football or baseball game. We talk about the trips. And we invariably think of some incident we'd not laughed about before. Or one we want to laugh about again.

But we don't sail together anymore. Beau's comfortable sailing with his wife and son. Oz has gone back to his girls and his other sports loves. My sailing adventures now are with Linda and other couples. Alan finds his escape in other ways.

We all know we *could* be out sailing together, continuing to discover. But we're not. Hard to figure, really. Maybe the four of us had fallen too much in love with the formula, so sure of its perfection we were no longer willing to shove our hand into life's box of chocolates and simply enjoy what we got.

It's damn certain there are moments when we're still being boys—it's just with other companions. When we can escape the utility bills, acting young and stupid does seem to be a universal gender-specific talent.

Risk-taking, in part, had driven us out there. But with all that comfort it got harder to face the uncertainty: sometimes the limo meets you at the door, sometimes you row your dinghy and pull the boat.

None of us have gone sailing with a new bunch of guys. I like to think it's merely that the memories are too pure.

Epilogue

The fireside is nice and there are those for whom it will be the ultimate Utopia, but the fireside is nicer still when you can remember the joys of an offshore passage and dream of the time when you can go out and do it again.

Ted Jones

This all may sound a bit like "Chevy Chase Goes Sailing." Sure, we talked dirty and told lies. Especially about women and sports. Guys do that, though there are no lies in this story: it all happened, pretty much like it appears here.

The truth of the matter is we never really overindulged, at least not before setting the hook; we never dragged an anchor; we never bumped anything, including the bottom; we never lost so much as a fork overboard (okay, except for the grill); we never had a problem we couldn't fix; we smoked all our cigars outside; and we returned every boat as clean as we found it.

Along the way our navigation and seamanship skills became first class. The trips forced us to really see one another, how we feel about almost everything. We may not remember all the details, but each of us certainly learned about himself and the others. Education took on a whole new meaning.

What we learned about new people and new cultures provide enduring memories. But the real lessons came from 24-7 togetherness. Okay, 24-5 some years. The bonds created by common experiences and uncommon sharing will long outlive the trips.

The nights we spent lying on the foredeck in total silence staring up at billions of stars are unforgettable. Magic, actually. So are the memories. Pulling on one of those shirts or playing the CDs brings an instant smile. And I can almost taste a rum-soaked brownie.

It really was all Tania's fault. She inspired us. She unknowingly got us to Florida to launch these adventures. And we did have adventures, even when we didn't seek them. The trips changed our lives. We got a helluva lot more than we bargained for, just chasing a dream.

Distant horizons are more inviting, tempting. We accomplished something: we dumped the ninny tag. Now we tell stories that, like Tania, capture the attention and imagination of the listener. I don't think we're inspirational. But we're better guys for having done it all.

Bibliography

Aebi, Tania, with Bernadette Brennan, *Maiden Voyage*. New York: Simon and Schuster, 1989

Caldwell, John, *Desperate Voyage*. Dobbs Ferry, NY: Sheridan House, 1949, 1991

McFarlane, Evelyn and James Saywell, *If . . . Questions for the Game of Life*. New York: Villard Books, 1995

Patterson, James and Peter de Jonge, *Miracle on the 17th Green*. London: Headliner Book Publishing, 1998

Scott, Nancy and Simon Scott, *The Cruising Guide to the Virgin Islands*, 8th ed. Dunedin, Florida: Cruising Guide Publications, Inc. 1996

Wouk, Herman, *Don't Stop the Carnival*. New York: Little, Brown, 1965, 1999

TOM WATKINS taught courses in leadership and dispute resolution to graduate business students and practicing managers for 30 years. He is currently president of *Solutions Associates*, an organization providing leadership, team building and negotiations workshops for a wide variety of organizations throughout the United States, sometimes through training aboard sailboats. He also serves as consultant and professor with a number of universities around the world, including recent assignments in Finland and New Zealand.

Tom has been an active sailor his whole adult life, owning trailer sailers whenever finances and water permit. He takes bareboat charter vacations every year (twice when his wife consents), in the most exotic locations he can find.

Other books of interest

IF *THE SHOE* FITS
Rae Ellen Lee
"...guided by love and sustained by humor...warm, human and very funny..."
—Linda Ridihalgh, editor, *Living Aboard*
"Lee shares her cruising adventures with deep personal
reflection and humor."—*Offshore*

BLOWN AWAY
Herb Payson
"'Getting away from it all' was not an impossible dream for Herb and
Nancy Payson, a California couple; they sold their belongings,
purchased a ketch, SEA FOAM, and sailed for the South Seas.... [Their]
story is a realistic portrait of an adventurous, enterprising family, with enough
sailing lore to satisfy most bluewater buffs."—*Publishers Weekly*

FLIRTING WITH MERMAIDS
John Kretschmer
"Not only has John Kretschmer lived a life wildly festooned with adventure, romance, and
outrageous characters—his reality outstripping our most Walter Mittyesque sea fantasies—now
he has gone and turned it all into a collection of yarns that incite yet more envy among those of us
stuck behind landbound computers. Not only can the sailor sail—through hurricanes and civil
wars—but the sailor can write. It's a hell of a read."—*Miami Herald*

THE BIGGEST BOAT I COULD AFFORD
Lee Hughes
This book tells Hughes' story as he makes his way up the Intracoastal Waterway, learning the
ways of the sea by trial and error. He is beached, swamped, wrecked, and he panics more than
once, but is sustained by the kindness of strangers. By journey's end, he has discovered what's
important to him—and conquered more than one fear.

BY WAY OF THE WIND
Jim Moore
"The best sailboat cruising book to come out in a long time."—*Washington Post*
"Far from simply amusing, this first-person narration tells about a couple with no sailing
experience but a commitment to a long-term dream and an addiction to the sea…
The book is filled with practical knowledge and ingenious do-it-yourself tips for
all amateur sailors."—*Yachting*

Sheridan House
America's Favorite Sailing Books
www.sheridanhouse.com